ngress Cataloging in Publication Number: 2006932858

59474-173-9

gapore
obe Garamond
Chuck U. Farley
y Moshe ben Bolt

North America by Chronicle Books
eet
CA 94105

3 2 1

treet
PA 19106
ks.com

D0031596

THE
EMP

Library of C

ISBN: 978-1

Printed in Si
Typeset in A
Designed by
Illustrations

Distributed
85 Second S
San Francisc

10 9 8 7 6 5

Quirk Books
215 Church
Philadelphia
www.quirkb

THE EVIL EMPIRE

101 WAYS THAT ENGLAND RUINED THE WORLD

By **STEVEN A. GRASSE**

Lay Historian and Voice of the American People

Foreword By

PENNY RIMBAUD

QUIRK BOOKS

PHILADELPHIA

FOREWORD

By PENNY RIMBAUD

E ver bothered to ask why the British speak English rather than British? The answer, simple and shameful as it is, is one that we English prefer to avoid. A mishmash of Latin, German, Norse, and French, the English language contains few words attributable to the original inhabitants of the British Isles: "penguin" being the most unlikely, "maggot" being the most unsavory (and a word that best describes the perception the English had of those early peoples). The English treatment of the early British people, language, and culture was contemptible from the start. But more of that (and penguins) later.

The Britain we speak of today is the net result of repeated invasions and subjugations of the first Britons. It began with the Romans, who hounded the woad-wearing natives to Britain's westernmost shores, thereby creating what later became the separate nations of Scotland, Wales, and Ireland. The Romans were followed by the Anglo-Saxons, who overpowered anyone silly enough to imagine they might still have some rightful claim to English soil. The Vikings then arrived, setting up a king and running off with the better-looking women. But it was the Normans who finally ensured that there wasn't a true Brit left standing on England's "green and pleasant land." The battle for England was over, but that of its Empire had only just begun.

First, acting more in their own interests than those of the English throne, the feudal overlords (most of whom were drunken French or Germans) placed their own people in servitude. When that didn't seem like enough, they invented the organized thuggery of governance, and parliamentary democracy set about brutally dominating the peoples of Scotland, Wales,

and Ireland, who, having been forced into submission, reluctantly accepted their place in what euphemistically became known as the United Kingdom. Those who tried to preserve the smallest scrap of native culture or mother tongue were systematically beaten or shipped across the globe. Either way, it was in the colonization of Britain that the ugly face of English imperialism first showed itself. But by who or what had the British finally been "united"? English kings and queens (foreigners one and all) and their toe-ragging servants in Parliament, legless on port, snoring on the benches, or, in the most severe cases, dead. And so there never was a British Empire. It was, and still is, an English Empire through and through.

It's easy to tell the true blue-blooded Englander. They're the ones with the shaved heads, the gold earrings, the football shirts advertising American mobile phones, or the collar and tie brigade stupid enough not to realize that they're sporting a readymade noose. They're the ones who still believe that England rules the waves, not realizing it did so by persistently waiving the rules. Fair play never entered the equation. It was death and destruction from the start. But that, of course, isn't how the history books tell it, preferring the "happy and glorious" deceits of the British National Anthem.

History is a cultural fiction controlled by those who create it. Was I ever told that my father's war against the Hun was a battle for capitalist supremacy? Of course not. I was told that it was a fight against evil—the persecution of Jews, which the English would have happily assented to had they been given half the chance. Was I told about the routine incarceration and torture of my fellow Brits, the Irish, or the wholesale slaughter of those Africans not deemed fit for the manacles of slavery? No, I was told the lie of a great Empire in which its peoples happily toiled for my benefit, of a benign democracy that listened to those peoples' voices and respected their lives, of a peace maintained through Christian fellowship. "God save our effing Queen."

The English think they invented everything. True, they didn't invent time, but, possession being nine-tenths of the law, they sure as hell think they own it. By a strange act of God, the zero line of longitude just so happens to run through the Royal Observatory at Greenwich, London. It's the original Ground Zero, another English first from which emanated the "war to start all wars": global dominance by the Crown of England.

Britain likes to claim that it's the world's oldest democracy, which simply means its inhabitants have been held in the thrall of one system of tyranny for longer than any other peoples on Earth. That's why in the face of authority they are so hopelessly submissive. Ever heard of a British Prime Minister being assassinated? The IRA took a shot at Margaret Thatcher, but, with God so firmly on her side, the bomb went off in the hotel bedroom at exactly the moment that she'd popped out to the loo. It was a mess-up, but if you want to see just how much of mess she could make, take a look at the Falklands debacle. It's Britain all over: a population of dirty-arsed, passive wool-heads following a small elite of self-important black-and-white stuffed shirts with about as much brain between them as, well, a penguin.

My dad said his war was a real war. He liberated Europe so that we Brits could live in peace until our leaders next decided we should die protecting their fortunes. Meanwhile, he took to playing golf at an exclusive club that didn't allow Jews. "But, Dad...." I once protested, but like Hitler (who as we know only had one), he'd lost his balls in a bunker. Dad wasn't anti-Semitic, he said so. It's just that like most every upright Englishman, he didn't much care for Jews, or come to that, Arabs, Asians, blacks, or indeed any foreigner. Being by nature xenophobic, the English detest their fellow Brits; after all, Taffy is a Welshman, and Taffy is a thief, the Irish have less up top than a half-baked potato, and the Scottish are even more penny-pinching than Shylock. It was that greatest of all Englishmen, Winston Churchill, who famously announced that "wops begin at Calais" (he would have

included the Scottish, Welsh, and the Irish if he hadn't needed them to be dying wholesale on his behalf on the frontlines of Europe).

What goes up must come down, and the "British Empire" is no exception. In its demise as a global power, England showed itself to be the nation of shopkeepers that Napoleon knew it to be. Having failed to restore international faith through her war against a flock of Argentinean sheep, Margaret Thatcher was forced to accept that the Empire was long past its sell-by date. True to her vocation as a grocer's daughter, she turned to flogging it off cheap to all comers, wops or not. Tony Blair, who's no more than a loud-mouthed barrow-boy, is making the most of what few used goods he has left at his disposal to gain political kudos by handing them over to George Bush. It's the sale of the century: proud past, golden future, or the rotting detritus of an empire which through its bullying arrogance once colored half the globe pink?

So, British Empire? What British Empire? Let's face it, the Empire's figure-head, Queen Elizabeth II, is no more than a German misanthropist ruling over an uncomfortable hodge-podge of disparate peoples whose only thing in common is a state of constant and considerable identity crisis. Put bluntly, Britain is a nation of cultural schizophrenics. And whilst we're at it, God isn't a Brit either, he's a Jew (but with clear English sympathies). No wonder, then, that Princess Diana was shunned by the royals after she'd been humped off by, dare I say it, a Muslim. And if you think that this might be getting just a little bit too controversial, read on. This book sets out to put the record straight. It gives the Empire its come-uppance, which is precisely what the British, but notably the English, deserve: a big dose of their own medicine.

I hope they choke on it.

—Penny Rimbaud

INTRODUCTION

I used to love traveling to London. The bustle of global commerce that echoes down London's charming cobblestone streets never fails to make me think of what New York City must have been like one hundred years ago. That was before America starting tearing down its history and encasing a few fragments in museum glass. Britain, on the other hand, experiences its past as a living part of its present. The smallest errand—like taking a ride on the Tube or eating a lunch of fish and chips—can be like taking a journey back in time.

A part of me wants to love all of the United Kingdom; because I'm an American, I've always looked up to the UK. The British seemed like older, wiser siblings—a little stiff maybe—but friends who have stuck by our side through thick and through thin.

Then, all of a sudden, just when America began to come into its own as a twenty-first century superpower, the British started picking on us. No longer do I feel warmth in the UK when I introduce myself as an American, but anger, bitterness, a hollow superiority, and most of all, intense jealousy. Over polite business luncheons, I've been told that my president is an idiot. That my countrymen are dolts for electing him. That America is responsible for ruining the world. After the premiere of my film "The Bikini Bandits Save Christmas" at the Raindance Film Festival in 2004, no one wanted to talk about my movie. All anyone wanted to talk about was the war in Iraq. In a few seasons, Britain's famous British sense of manners and decorum vanished before my eyes.

I'm a patriotic man. There's only so much abuse I can take. And while I hate to point fingers, Britain is in no position to be blaming the United States for the world's problems, problems that *they themselves created in the first place.* Now, having seen too many a smug Englishman drag the name of my country through the mud, I've decided to fight back.

I've found it difficult to talk sense into a Briton once he's taken that second sip of gin. Maybe that is why so many British are alcoholics. They drink to forget what they've done to the world. Don't believe me? Try ducking into the nearest pub and explaining to some of those Tommy Atkinses how . . .

- The British crown profited from slavery and backed the Confederacy
- British soldiers massacred thousands of defenseless Africans with machine guns
- King Arthur lived in a cave, if in fact he lived at all
- British foreign policy, not American foreign policy, created the messes in Iraq, Israel, and Afghanistan
- Queen Elizabeth II is the direct descendant of cannibalistic Druids

You'll see what I mean. The British are terrible listeners. I don't blame them. They are a prideful people, and the truths I am about to reveal may simply be too painful for them to ever fully acknowledge. But the simple language and easily grasped illustrations of this book are intended to make the truth about the British legacy apparent, even to a boorish lout in a state of complete inebriation.

Unlike the Germans and the Japanese, the British have never been confronted with the fact that their past is not as innocent as their historians would have them believe. This is why they feel so comfortable arrogantly blaming everything on the United States. Is my country to blame? To answer this question, I usually deploy what I call the Bathroom Analogy. Say John Bull walks into a public bathroom. Having had a traditional English breakfast of lamb guts, and fried potatoes, he proceeds to clog up the toilet with an enormous stinking dump. He then walks out without

saying a word. In walks Uncle Sam, ready to take an imperial shit of his own. He notices the toilet is clogged and starts going at it with the plunger. It may appear to those waiting outside that Uncle Sam is causing the delay, when really, as you'll see, he's dealing with the mess that John Bull left behind.

Completely documenting the ill effects Britain has had on our planet is a project that would take a lifetime to complete. My hope is that this book will point the way toward a truer history of Britain by shedding light on some of the country's darker areas. I can only hope that others will follow the trails of inquiry I have blazed herein to their ultimate destination.

Over the next few pages, I will take you on an ignominious journey, a two-thousand-year tale of plunder, pillage, murder, and deceit. You will see villages ransacked, native cultures destroyed, flawed men held up as royalty, and homicidal inventions perfected by devious minds. You will wonder how Britain made it through the nineteenth and twentieth centuries with its reputation intact while Germany, France, and Russia all went down in flames. You will never think of tea in the same way again.

You will likely be left asking, "What can I do?," and for this, I have an answer. The Evil Empire owes us. It owes us big. By my calculations, Britain's total debt to the world runs well into the trillions. I don't intend to let this debt go.

At the end of this book, you'll find a bill I intend to present, in person, to Queen Elizabeth II. I intend to stand up and demand that Britain make things right.

I ask that you stand with me.

—Steven A. Grasse

THEY THINK THEY OWN THE "ENGLISH" LANGUAGE

The linguistic vanity of the Englishman is apparent in every word he speaks. Every nuanced syllable is relished—every lilt and pause is supposed to subtly convey class and pedigree like the colored stripes on a regimental tie. The English are so in love with the sight and sound of their own words that even their signs are needlessly verbose, never using a word where two or three will do. There's "Way Out" for "Exit," "Water Closet" for "Bathroom," and "Kill Your Speed" for "55."

Even though the roots of the English language go back to Germany and Mesopotamia, not Britain, Oxford snobs would have us believe that their special definitions and word histories as set down in the *Oxford English Dictionary* are the "last word" on what sounds denote what meanings, despite the well-documented fact that one of the dictionary's most dutiful volunteer contributors did his work in an insane asylum and wound up cutting off his own penis.

Thus, we shouldn't be too surprised that *genocide* did not come into common usage among historians until after Germany—one of Britain's enemies—committed one. By enforcing an intellectual cartel over the use of words, Britain has managed to whitewash most English-language versions of their country's sordid history. Until now.

THEY ARE
SECRETLY PAGAN

Deep in the woods of Brittany and Wales, long after the Middle East was basking in the glow of sane monotheism, Druid priests led early Britons in pagan ceremonies. Fires were lit and danced around. Cernunnos, the elk god of masculine virility, was worshiped. And worst of all, according to extensive archaeological evidence, live human beings were sacrificed to the pagan gods. The Druid priests held the country in the palm of their bloodstained hands, paying no taxes, building no temples, and controlling the superstitious and primitive early English mind through fire, fear, and tall tales. They left nothing behind in the form of writing or ritual, just piles of innocent bones buried beneath altars.

You might think the British would be ashamed of this murderous pagan past, but no, they *celebrate* the bloodshed of history is hidden behind a whitewashed wall of kitsch. Tours are given of sacred pagan sites. Druid symbolism appears in tattoo art and on the drum kits of famous bands like Led Zeppelin. Games like Dungeons and Dragons make parents believe that sorcery and necromancy are suitable playtime activities for their children. The Ancient Order of Druids survives to this day, observing solstices at Stonehenge and even appearing in the London telephone directory. While allegations of human sacrifice are enough to make South American and African natives into "savages" in the eyes of colonial British historians, their own record of religious killings has gone more or less ignored.

THEY MORE OR LESS CASTRATED SCOTLAND

The British Isles consist of England, Ireland, Wales, and Scotland, and could not have come to dominate the world had England, seat of the Evil Empire, not essentially enslaved the other three isles, seizing upon the raw grunt manpower of the Irish, the farming skills of the Welsh, and the savage warriors of the Scottish Highlands.

At the dawn of the twentieth century, with World War I approaching, poor Ireland was providing 70 percent of the conscripts for the British Army. Scotland, meanwhile, was supplying at least 80 percent of the balls. Their soldiers trained with the traditional games on fields of heather and heath, tossing one-hundred-pound tree trunks and hammers. Two hundred years of attempting revolutions against the English had honed their guerilla tactics to a fine point.

It's sad that conniving imperial cowards would twist the strength of a freedom-loving people to serve their megalomanical ends. Sad, but not surprising.

THEY TRIED TO DRAG
CHRIST TO LONDON

The sorest spot in the British version of history is the fact that
Christ spent his life in the Middle East. British zealots have tried
all manner of brazen strategies to bring Christ to Britain after the fact.
Before soccer games, fans sing the song "Jerusalem," originally a poem
by William Blake. It's Britain's unofficial national anthem, and it
openly attempts to perpetuate the false notion that Christ's own holy
sandals trod upon the Isles:

> *And did those feet in ancient time*
> *Walk upon England's mountains green?*
> *And was the holy Lamb of God*
> *On England's pleasant pastures seen?*

Did those feet walk upon England's mountains green? Jesus' feet?
Absolutely not. Yet this lie was far less damaging than the madness of
the Crusades, a campaign instigated by the British crown and other
European rulers to take the Holy Land—lands to which they had no
right—back from Muslim rule. After obtaining the blessings of the
Pope for their pointless campaigns, they soldiered forth with battal-
ions of armored warriors, all bored stiff and armed to the teeth.

THEY ADOPTED A ROMAN
AS THEIR SAINT
AND BLAMED PAST MISDEEDS
ON A GIANT LIZARD

There are few places where England's lack of authentic heroes is more apparent than its flag, the so-called Flag of Saint George. England claims Saint George as their national saint, yet he was born in Palestine, not anywhere near England. Like King Arthur, Robin Hood, and all the rest of Britain's heroes (some imported, some invented), Saint George was made an Englishman during the Middle Ages, when England's lack of pedigree made her ashamed to stand beside her proud Continental brethren. The traditional Saint George was venerated not as a hero, but as a martyr who refused to join in the persecution of Christians under Roman rule.

Perhaps finding this story too passive for their would-be national hero, the English invented the tale of George and the dragon, in which a dragon terrorizes an English village, demanding a human sacrifice of one fair maiden per day. Eventually it is the princess' turn to go, and the king calls upon George, a wandering knight, to dispatch the dragon, thus making himself the flag's legendary namesake. And so England named her flag for a fairytale hero who was neither a knight, nor a slayer of dragons, nor even truly English.

THEY RELISH
COLLECTING
TAXES

What do you think was the very first thing William the Conqueror did after assuming the throne of England in 1066? Help his new subjects build new huts? Get the mud out of the drinking water? Try to stop the deadly spread of dysentery? No, centuries before the crown started to provide anything in the way of services to its subjects, it was already eagerly tallying up their possessions and collecting taxes. William's Domesday book, a comprehensive census of every property, man, pig, ox, and chicken in England, marked a crucial transition from the early days of princely tribute paid out to a local strongman to the modern system of taxation we own today, where the government shows up once a year to take a bite out of the wealth we've all worked so hard to accumulate.

Today, the *Guinness Book of World Records* and *Encyclopedia Britannica* fool us into thinking there's nothing untoward about the British fetish for books, ledgers, and record keeping, but the Domesday book shows us that the uncontrollable avarice of the taxman is what's behind this regulatory urge. Half a millennium before the Evil Empire started its march across the globe, the model was already in place: The people make, the crown takes.

THEY CUT OFF THE HEAD OF WILLIAM "BRAVEHEART" WALLACE

Few films have managed to capture the essence of the English conscience as effectively as *Braveheart*. This epic masterpiece shows us how centuries before the Evil Empire would seek to subdue the noblest savages of the world, they got their practice battling the ancient Scottish tribes, gradually eroding their will to form one United Kingdom.

The English had yearned to subdue the Scots since building Stonehenge, a monument of three giant stones enslaving an outlying ring of smaller ones. The big stones represent Scotland, England, and Wales. The small stones are the rest of the world. That, in a nutshell, is the English worldview, a paranoid desire for control that simply can't put up with warriors secure enough in their masculinity to paint their faces and wear skirts on the battlefield.

Throughout the 1200s and 1300s, these Scottish warriors fought mightily to retain control of their emerald turf in several wars of independence. The English were so incensed by William Wallace, the stout Scot played by Mel Gibson, that they prolonged his torture and execution for as long as possible, first hanging him, then removing his genitals, then ripping his live body into four bloody pieces. It wasn't until the eighteenth century that England finally managed to bring Scotland to heel, an appetizer that served to whet her newfound appetite for territory and subjects.

THEY HATE FREEDOM

Freedom is the word that got the Minutemen to take their rifles down from the mantle and assemble in the streets of Lexington and Concord. It's the word that gets American hearts beating and ready to brawl. And it's the word that hurts an Englishman's ears almost as much as *bloody*.

The Englishman doesn't like hearing about freedom because he doesn't have any. Today's Britain gives the appearance of being a free and open society, but anyone who has lived there for a significant length of time knows that this is not the case. Every car that enters downtown London is photographed by government cameras, which capture the license plates and send the owners bills. Commit a more serious transgression, and you'll be hauled into a private interrogation chamber by one of the most brutal intelligence organizations in the world. That's Scotland Yard, a gang of pug-faced louts who have been disappearing cantankerous Irishmen for decades. Worst of all are the ASBOs, short for Anti-Social Behavior Orders. Any friend or neighbor annoyed by a fellow Brit's behavior can go before a judge and demand an ASBO to stop you from throwing parties, making noise, even smoking out on the stoop. Break the ASBO, and you risk being sent to prison for up to five years. Neighbors slapped Alexander Maut, an eighty-seven-year-old man from Merseyside, with an ASBO to stop him from saying sarcastic things to their visitors.

In America, we indulge such curmudgeonly behavior, for it reminds us of the rugged individualism from which we sprang. Britain prizes conformity above all and uses the law to beat the slightest deviation from the community's standard of uptight propriety.

THEY THINK KINGS AND QUEENS ARE BETTER THAN THE REST OF US

Why do you think America's Founding Fathers had to write "all men are created equal" into the Constitution? Was that something they took for granted? Something they were used to under British rule? No way! The idea of equality under the law may seem completely obvious to us today, so obvious that we take it for granted, but George Washington, Thomas Jefferson, and all the rest wrote it into the Constitution because they knew how painful it is to bow down to be judged by your daddy's coat of arms instead of by your character's content.

And who exactly does the Prime Minister minister to? The British people? Hate to break it to you pal, but it's the Queen. To this day, the British political universe revolves around an old lady who didn't do a lick of work to get there. Now, the progressive lad down at the pub will tell you that the royal family is kept around for purely ceremonial reasons, sort of like the giant Mickey Mouse balloon that floats down Fifth Avenue in New York every Thanksgiving and spends the rest of the year mothballed in a warehouse. If that were the case, would British taxpayers willingly pay £37 million each year for her royal retinue, wardrobe, and upkeep? Would they allow her to live, rent-free, in a sprawling palace defended by redcoats in unnecessarily opulent beaver-fur hats? Would they append the words "Her Majesty" onto the names of government bureaus, fighting planes, and sailing ships? Would they have stood aside while Prince Charles committed marital

offenses that mortal politicians would be pilloried over?

No, clearly something far more insidious is at work in the relationship between the British people and the monarch. It's more than tradition. It's worship. The British mind desperately needs a strict hierarchy to function. It needs to put a crown on an old lady simply for the sake of having something to bow down before.

THEIR COUNTRY HAS TOO MANY FLAGS AND TOO MANY NAMES

Many of my countrymen use the terms England, Britain, and the United Kingdom interchangeably, as though they were as synonymous as the United States of America, the Union, and, simply, America. Not so. The Evil Empire's three names are as nuanced as a Venn diagram and as nested as a set of Russian dolls, the largest of which is the United Kingdom, which is actually short for the United Kingdom of Great Britain and Northern Ireland.

Take out Northern Ireland and you've got Great Britain, "great" because it is three nations in one—Scotland, Wales, and England— each of which has its own parliament, ministerial authority, and flag. That's the Union Jack, which looks like a red cross on top of a red "X." It is actually three flags in one—the red cross of England on top of the white "X" of Scotland and the red "X" of Ireland. (Wales, as usual, gets shortchanged.)

Compare this to the U.S. flag—fifty stars for fifty states. All united. All equal. The UK, on the other hand, is like the Soviet Union of old. It is "united" in name only. Everyone knows Wales, Ireland, and Scotland are England's obedient bitches.

THEY REWROTE THE BIBLE

What could be more arrogant than strutting around with a crown and a scepter, pretending that thanks to God you are on a higher plane of being than your fellow man? How about rewriting the word of God and putting your name on it?

That's exactly what King James I did in 1611, when, unhappy with the stilted style and moldy prose of the Geneva Bible, he commissioned a brand-new version chock-full of thees, thous, and all the rest of the latest slang. Too lazy and uneducated to do the translation himself, he hired a bevy of academics from Oxford and Cambridge to do all the heavy lifting and then slapped his name on the result, a bible that wasn't any more accurate than its predecessor, but wound up being cast in a charmingly poetic brand of seventeenth-century English that we associate today with Shakespeare, ruffled collars, and the like.

And so on its suposed beauty rather than its merits, the King James Bible has survived, even spawning a movement of King James–only fanatics (Baptists, mostly) who maintain that the king's committees were divinely inspired, as tuned into God's still small voice as Moses at the top of Mount Sinai. If you believe that, let me tell you about how I'm the living reincarnation of King James himself, and all the back taxes you owe me.

THEY BURNED JOAN OF ARC AT THE STAKE

In 1428, a sixteen-year-old French girl had visions from God. Following God's divine instructions to the letter, she wound up leading a pack of oppressed Frenchmen into battle against their chain-mailed British imperial overlords. Atop her horse, in the midst of combat, she was struck with an arrow. Demonstrating almost super-human valor, she ripped it from her shoulder and returned to the front of the French line to lead the charge. And there's more. Faced with death by fire, she refused to recant. Let's just say that Joan of Arc did more with each minute of her nineteen years than Paris Hilton could do with a thousand lifetimes.

In America, we call such behavior *talent*. We lavish all the money and attention we can on it, praying that it will continue to blossom. When we're blessed to encounter an otherworldly star like Michael Jordan, we hail him as a god and name shoes after him, even if he occasionally feels like staying up all night playing blackjack the night before the big game.

In England, such standout behavior goes by another name: *heresy*. Heresy is a capital offense, grounds for your teenaged body to be thrown in the flames and burnt to a crisp not once but thrice, so that no relics of your saintly life will remain. Joan won out in the end—following her death, France freed itself from the Evil Empire's grimy tentacles, and the Catholic Church rewarded her with posthumous sainthood. But what might she have accomplished had she lived to see fifty or seventy? Thanks to the British, we'll never know.

THEY SUPPORT PIRACY

Well not piracy exactly. Queen Elizabeth would never endorse such a thing. She did, however, issue what's known as a "letter of marque" to certain sailors, giving them permission to loot the ships of any enemy nation, particularly those of the Spanish, whose hated armada was keeping the Evil Empire from the global dominance it sought. So a pirate was a pirate, unless he was friends with the Queen. Then he was known by the dignified title of *privateer*. (Change the letters around and you get *rev pirate!*)

The most famous privateer was Sir Francis Drake, who got used to the sight of blood by slaying six hundred Irish on Rathlin Island. In the sixteenth century you could win medals for performing such hideous deeds, and two years later Queen Elizabeth granted Drake permission to start scouring the globe for booty. Over the next eight years, he would travel around the world, sinking Spanish ships wherever he met them, seizing their gold, and sending their crews' bodies down into the briny deep. His naval campaign scored its greatest achievement in 1588, when he finally defeated Spain's armada.

So pay no attention to the jittery Brits when they criticize the CIA's use of wild-eyed soldiers of fortune. Four hundred years before, their own Queen deployed some of the most dastardly villains on the high seas. Whether it's 1588 or 2006, you can't build an empire without some tough guys to man the cannons.

THEY TOOK THE CHRIST
OUT OF CHRISTIANITY

Since the dawn of time, kings have laid down with whatever fair maiden they please, consequences be damned. In this respect, Henry VIII was just like any other king, frequently releasing his princely loads into harems of mistresses kept on palace grounds for that precise purpose.

But when the loins of Henry's wife, Queen Catherine, proved sterile ground for germinating a royal heir, Henry decided he wanted to promote one of his mistresses, the bulldog-faced but seductive Anne Boleyn, to the throne. This was the 1530s, and to get a divorce back then you had to write a letter to the Pope in Rome. The Pope wasn't having it, so, for the sake of liberating his royal sperm, Henry established his new Anglican Church as the official Church of England. Any religious officials or journalists who dissented from the crown— those who pointed out the hypocrisy of his decision—were arrested, tortured, and killed.

A few years later, Henry grew tired of his new wife. He falsely accused her of incest as a pretext for killing her and making room on the bloodied royal mattress for his third wife. So say what you will about the Catholic Church—the Anglican Church was founded by one of the most unchristian men in history, a lustful and bitter barbarian. But someone in England must be into it, because this historical aberration is still around nearly five hundred years later.

THEY TRIED TO MEASURE AND CONTROL THE UNIVERSE THROUGH SCIENCE

The year is 1666. After spending a decade inundating your brain with mathematics, astronomy, and the jagged theoretical edges of Aristotelian science, you're kicking back by enjoying a sunny day beneath a shady tree. Then—plunk!—something falls on your head. An apple! And then, the epiphany hits you: *With the falling of this apple I can explain the entire natural world.*

Fat chance, Sir Isaac Newton. While your calculus and your physics have done a reasonably good job of explaining the behavior of apple-sized objects, your theories are next to worthless when it comes to describing the behavior of microscopic particles and giant solar systems. You can't begin to explain fractals, chaos theory, quarks, or turbulence. You can't even tell us what the weather is going to be like tomorrow.

And, as innumerable natural disasters indicate, any success we've had at controlling the natural world through Newtonian views has been fleeting and vain. Instead of trying to dominate nature through precise and constant measurement, contemporary scientists are saying we should learn to weave our lives into harmony with the patterns in our natural environment.

It's a pretty obvious lesson, one that we might have figured out hundreds of years ago had Sir Isaac Newton not sent us down a blind alley. His few genuine contributions were grossly inflated by Oxford dons to make Britain seem like God's gift to science.

THEY DEMEAN "PRIMITIVE" CULTURE IN THE AMERICAS

Around 200 BC, while the Romans were building aqueducts and the Greeks were perfecting the foundations of science, the English were busying themselves pushing dirt into circular mounds and undertaking other shamefully useless projects. Among these was the Cerne Abbas giant, depicting a man 180 feet tall, near Dorset. The giant is formed by a trench carved into a hillside. He is carrying a giant knobbed club. He has a rock-hard penis, pointing straight up, that's thirty feet long.

Way to be a mature civilization, guys. Instead of covering up the giant and his monstrous Lord Nelson, the people of this shire scrub out the phallic ditch every seven years to keep him looking as fresh as the day the Druids made him. No one is sure exactly what the giant was used for. Some have speculated he marked a place where orgies or fertility rites were held.

The apparent uselessness of Stonehenge, similarly, has befuddled historians looking to find some practical motive in the ancient Englishman's Neolithic rock gardens. Why would ancient men have spent more than 240 of their years building something with no apparent purpose? The pyramids, after all, were tombs, and the greatest of Maya temples served some astrological functions. We can only conclude that the beliefs of the ancient Briton were so alien to the way we experience the world today that they are beyond interpretation.

THEY ENSLAVED THE GLOBE TO GET THEIR TEA FIX

I'm not even going to address the subject of how utterly girlish it is to build your culture around the ritual drinking of a glass of hot water flavored with exotic leaves. That's silly, sure, but not wrong. Not evil.

What's evil is using these cute little leaves as the foundation of your entire foreign policy and economy, which is exactly what the British Empire did. Along with silk, cotton, and indigo, tea was the main commodity that drove the British East India Company to make India its slave and China its captive. Tea was the reason tens of thousands of acres were razed; the backs of able-bodied men were broken working them. All for tea. A *drink*. Back at home, tea captains steered their ships along the Thames in London to the cheers of assembled crowds, while hostesses queued up to obtain the latest mix of Darjeeling and Earl Grey for their silver-plated pots and parlor tables. By the Industrial Revolution, factory owners discovered that a brief tea break and accompanying boost of sugar and caffeine would give their employees the juice to work long into the night.

Wherever tea is quaffed, there are men in chains. Small wonder then that the glorious American Revolution began with the East India Company's tea getting tossed into Boston Harbor. Throwing those foul leaves of oppression into the water was the equivalent of giving King George himself the finger. The moment those crates hit the water, it was on.

THEY DAWDLE THE HOURS AWAY WITH CRICKET, AMONG OTHER FOOLISH GAMES

After a long day of wiping out indigenous peoples and groveling at the feet of their local viceroy, there's nothing colonial Brits enjoyed more than pouring a cold gin and tonic and playing some sort of game. It can't be too strenuous—pudding-bellied barons in safari suits and pith helmets have to stand a fighting chance, as do inbred royals.

Card games like bridge and whist fit the bill, as do backgammon, darts, and other pub games. But the strangest and laziest of all British pastimes is cricket, a "sport" that requires so much gear and so little ability that one would be forgiven for thinking it was invented by a manufacturer of sporting goods.

Men in white sweaters and baggy pantaloons lope back and forth between two wickets. The game is so soft that players routine rack up hundreds of runs in a single game, a feat known as a "century." The winner is the one who knows the rules best and deploys them to his advantage, and who manages to stay awake through the game's dreary progress.

THEY SPREAD THE PLAGUE WITH THEIR BAD HYGIENE

The Black Death hit England in the middle of the fourteenth century, killing off nearly one-third of the country's population. Every morning, the village undertaker would roll his cart down each street, ringing his bell and bellowing "Bring out your dead!" Priests, farmers, even powerfully built blacksmiths would take ill and retire to bed, where they would break out in oozing sores. Days later, they would be dead.

England wasn't the only country to fall victim to the plague—beginning in Italy, it spread across the whole of Europe, killing off thirty-five million in all. But one would think such losses would have made the British realize that the plague was caused by rats and fleas and furthered by medieval hygiene habits. Not so. Instead, they relied upon the advice of alchemists and lay physicians who treated their wounds with leeches and wasps, gave them foul-tasting tinctures to drink, cast a few ineffectual spells, and otherwise left them to die. The priestly classes believed the plague meant God was angry. They tried to appease him with hairshirts and self-flagellation—anything but lathering up a little soap and water. To your medieval Brit, cleanliness was a fate worse than death.

THEY BELIEVE IN DRAGONS, SEA MONSTERS, AND OTHER CREATURES

The British have long associated their beloved monarchy with the Leviathan, a giant and imaginary fish, a colossal serpent of the sea who breathes fire and snacks on ships. His blood is as hot and orange as lava. His fierce heart shakes the deep like a volcano. As the Book of Job puts it, "His breath kindleth coals, and a flame goeth out of his mouth."

For centuries, even though no such creature had ever been spotted with human eyes, fearful British mapmakers drew Leviathans in any unknown body of water, both to break up the great expanse of empty unmapped oceans and as a kind of warning sign, telling British sailors never to venture too far out into the unknown.

Thus, while Spanish and Portuguese explorers blazed across the seas from continent to continent, the mythological Leviathan kept British captains tacking close to shore. Unable to muster the courage needed to make any successful or daring ocean voyage, the cautious Brits would take another hundred years to master their fear of the all-powerful Leviathan and join the rest of Europe on the high seas.

THEY CONCEAL THEIR CAVEMAN PAST WITH FALSE HISTORIES

British civilization didn't have much going for it until the fourteenth or fifteenth century. You had the dark Druidic caveman ages followed by the dark and priestly Middle Ages, interrupted by the brief period of progress made under Roman rule. This caused the Evil Empire no small amount of shame when they set about conquering Egypt, Babylon, China, and other civilizations that had genuinely glorious pasts.

To compensate, they started telling stories. To forget about the primitive backwardness of the Dark Ages, they told the story of King Arthur and his charming band of knights. To conceal the fact that they were on the outskirts of the ancient world, they invented a tale about Christ having paid a visit during his time on Earth. A certain hawthorn bush growing outside Glastonbury Abbey is supposed to have been planted in ancient times by one of Christ's disciples. All bunk.

At this same time, while British civilization existed only in caves and fiction, the Aztecs were doing astronomy and calculus and the Chinese were building a wall so big you can see it from the moon. But who needs a real glorious past when it's so easy to make one up?

THEY MAKE TIME FOR TEA

I've already weighed in on the evils of the tea commodity itself, but what of the time wasted in its preparation and consumption? What of the ritual? What of the human attention diverted, the hours filled with idle chatter and the listless dipping of scones into cups of Earl Grey?

Were the English to waste their leisure hours on such activities, it would be shocking enough, but for them to set aside as much as an hour of every workday for the performance of an out-of-date imperialist ritual embodies at least two of the seven deadly sins—pride and sloth. Let's throw gluttony in there as well, for were it not for the designated snack times pioneered by Thomas Twinning and the rest of the tea lords, today's worker wouldn't be carrying an extra fifteen pounds of compressed Snickers nougat around his waistline.

Listen up, Britain. Here's how work works: You're either working, or you're goofing off. What you don't do is drop everything at four o'clock in the afternoon and sit around eating cookies until evening comes. If everyone took tea, society would collapse. In America, we idolize the hustlers who work all day and all night. We don't need a special break or ritual to drink our coffee—we do it at our desks! When we want to relax, we go home! Slacking off while on the clock is not my cup of tea.

THEY HOOKED THE CHINESE ON OPIUM

What could be worse than looking out your window and seeing a drug dealer on the corner, peddling his narcotic wares to every passerby? How about a drug dealer who sets up camp on your doorstep and pummels your walls with musket fire and cannonballs until you finally allow him to sell drugs from inside your very home?

Grisly stuff, I know, but it's exactly what Britain did to China during the nineteenth-century opium wars. The Brits began exporting opium into China in the 1700s to help fund their addiction to another powerful drug—tea. But while tea is good for little more than a mild afternoon buzz, opium (much like heroin, its trendily pierced grandchild) will wrap you up in a cocoon of irresistible pleasure as it rots you from the inside out.

Such was the fate of the estimated fourteen million Chinese who were hooked on opium by 1900. Their lost livelihoods and broken homes amounted to little more than so many hash marks on John Bull's ledger. Dauguong, the Chinese emperor, was so fed up with the Brits' drug-dealing ways that in 1839 he expelled the British opium traders from his country. They soon returned with gunboats, willing to use violence to keep the Chinese hooked. After enduring such a trauma at the hands of the Evil Empire, is it any wonder China eventually succumbed to the siren song of Communism?

THEY MAKE GOOD MEN INTO BUTLERS, AND THEY MAKE BUTLERS INTO SLAVES

Anyone who has witnessed the degrading servitude of butlerdom up close knows why Brits slyly call it the world's "second oldest profession." For just as prostitution callously takes a common woman's virtue and puts it up for sale, so does butlery coarsen masculine virtue by taking lower- and middle-class men, dressing them up like penguins, and making them believe that all they are good for is managing wine cellars and laying doilies down on silver tea services.

In this way, butlery serves to reinforce Britain's rigid class hierarchy by isolating the most useful and intelligent members of the lower classes in a place where the aristocracy can keep careful watch on them, all while indoctrinating them with the belief that they exist only to serve. Meanwhile children of the aristocracy learn at an early age that they will never be called upon to do real work, and they quickly spoil into perfectly useless twits.

The dark side of butlery was even more evident during the height of the Evil Empire, when the strongest and most enterprising local men were made into footmen and majordomos, completely robbed of their dignity but paid for a month's work what they might otherwise make in a year. Britain's butler neuroses were on prominent display during the trial of Princess Diana's butler, Paul Burrell, who was accused of stealing heirlooms from her estate. The tabloids were awash with accusations of betrayal and secret royal liaisons. Burrell was cleared, but not before the world had been reminded that Britain is a country whose leaders demand constant pampering. And to think they still criticize Americans for slavery, which we abolished, while butlery is alive and well on their shores.

THEY CREATED THE FIRST VERY STUPID AND VERY VIOLENT PUPPET SHOW FOR CHILDREN

The blowhards and editorialists like to complain that the entertainments we give our children—the video games, the comic books, the Saturday morning cartoons—are debased, overly crude, and/or violent; that they somehow fail to embody the values we wish to impart to the younger generation. These statements are infected with a nostalgia for the "good old days" lived under the watchful gaze and traditional nanny values of the Evil Empire, when kids read Chaucer and studied Greek and Latin.

Or so we are made to believe. Yet hundreds of years before tykes gathered 'round a glowing box to watch Tom the cat and Jerry the mouse dismember one another, a hook-nosed gentleman named Punch regularly beat the living crap out of his innocent companion, Judy. With his long walking stick (resembling the crude club of Stone Age Brits), the puppet Punch inflicted his painful wrath on babies, crocodiles, even police officers. He was known to beat Death himself to death.

Children, under intense pressure from their overbearing Victorian parents, were forced to laugh at these cruel spectacles, and ever since, children's entertainment has followed a degenerate path of puppets inflicting vicious assaults on one another. Only an imperialist could find this sort of thing funny.

THEY THINK TERRORISTS ARE HEROES

What would the American people do to a man who plotted to blow up Congress and kill the president? Would we name a national holiday after him? Would we celebrate him in pop songs, comic books, and on the silver screen?

Unlikely. Consider John Wilkes Booth. Osama bin Laden. Ted Kaczynski. A terrorist is a terrorist and a traitor is a traitor, whether they were born in Pakistan or Palo Alto. Americans prize loyalty above all else. We despise traitors with a special hatred reserved for the lowest of the low—cattle thieves, child molesters, and other scum who threaten to undermine the virtuous foundations on which America is built.

What then, are we to make of the twisted love the Brits have shown for Guy Fawkes, whose Gunpowder Plot sought to blow up both houses of Parliament, kill every member of the House of Lords, and assassinate King James I? In the days after his crime in 1605, Fawkes was widely considered a scoundrel. He was tortured, executed, and the people burned him in effigy in the streets. A couple of hundred years after that, the anniversary of Fawkes's scheme was used as an excuse to instigate anti-Catholic hatred, and the Pope was burned in effigy alongside Guy. Today, the event has the status of a national holiday. The whole country sings and dances around the bonfire. Kids munch on special candies. Such displays give the impression that terrorism is a laughing matter. They are in poor taste, and you won't be seeing them stateside on September 11 in 2101 or 2501.

BRITISH MEN ARE A LITTLE LIMP IN THE WRIST, IF YOU GET MY MEANING

I have nothing against homosexuals, nor have I found homosexuality to be any more or less prevalent in the UK than it is anywhere else. I do, however, believe that upper class British males exhibit a peculiar chumminess and an aversion to hard work that could be characterized as, shall we say, fey. This likely has its origins in their schoolboy days, when lessons were punctuated by stern spankings from the lecturer's ruler and furtive cloakroom gropings.

For hundreds of years, British homosexuals had to keep their orientation secret under restrictive sumptuary laws. Intended to maintain the established social order, these laws regulated everything from the right to wear lace cuffs to certain textiles and dyes, which were to be donned only by the nobility. From the early 1500s on, English authorities punished sodomy or "buggery" by death, and were still stringing their gay countrymen up on the gallows pole as late as 1833. Even the leaders of British society eschewed the company of women, preferring to spend their evenings nursing a glass of port at homosocial private clubs.

Seems contradictory, but this sort of do-as-I-say-not-as-I-do repression is at the heart of Victorian morality. If only these clubmen had come to terms with their own urges, the Stonewall riot might never have been necessary. Far more civilized were the ancient Romans, who found that embracing homosexuality made their armies of lovers fight even more ferociously while keeping the birth rate from swallowing up their giant empire's overstretched resources.

THEY'RE RUN BY
THE HOUSE OF LORDS
(AKA THE AXIS OF WEEVILS)

The British tradition of inherited aristocratic rule disappeared with the horse-drawn buggy and the top hat. Whatever's left is purely ceremonial in nature. That's the story you'll hear from the Anglophiles whose broad, tweed-encased bottoms fill the leather club chairs of America's country clubs and university faculties, and it's wrong.

Britain never fully adopted the norms of equality under the law and reasoned republican rule that took root in North America and throughout the rest of Western Europe. Out of the 713 members of the House of Lords—Britain's equivalent of the United States Senate—not one was elected. Five hundred and nintey-five serve for life. Ninety-two are barons, counts, and other nobles who inherited their posts and will likely pass them on to their own children. Twenty-six are prominent clergymen known as "Lords Spiritual," who serve to add further incestuous intrigue to British relations between church and state. The House of Lords is far more than ceremonial. It can write law, sometimes serves as the highest court in the land, and can delay legislation from the democratically elected House of Commons for up to a year.

It's true that we Americans have our own dynasties—Adamses, Roosevelts, Kennedys, Bushes, and the like—but at least these trust-fund babies actually had to go out and win some votes to assume their fathers' offices. In Britain, just show your silver spoon at the door and you'll be given a seat at the table of royal power.

THEY TAKE CREDIT
FOR EVERYTHING

It's disturbing to see just how many scourges, plagues, and twisted inventions have sprung from the soil of the Evil Empire. Perhaps sensing their shabby showing, British historians are always quick to write their country into the record as a forerunner of the virtuous, the innovative, and the generally worthwhile.

For example, the Magna Carta, a thirteenth-century deal worked out between King John and a council of jealous barons, is often cited as a prototype for the freedoms granted by the United States Constitution, even though it makes no mention of equal justice under law or the various freedoms and rights of speech, assembly, religion, privacy, bearing arms, and speedy, fair trials that Americans hold so dear and have since become the gold standard of freedom around the world. All the Magna Carta says is that King John's power is not infinite. He can't dictate what the church does; he can't confiscate lands from felons; he can't appoint unqualified men as his royal officers; and he had to give accused parties a rough-and-ready thirteenth-century form of due process before finding them guilty, drawing and quartering them, chopping off their heads, or taking whatever other royal liberties he liked with their guilty bodies.

You call that freedom? The Magna Carta did little to delimit the king's powers. Rather, it ensured that the British monarchy would survive for another eight hundred years by taking away its most primitive and tribal aspects and spreading its bounty among the barons and the rest of the aristocracy.

THEY TRIED TO TAKE OVER ANTARCTICA

Who would ever want sovereign claim to a strategically worthless patch of frozen land at the southern end of the globe? Who would care about having authority over a few thousand penguins and the glaciers on which they nest? Land-hungry imperial gluttons, that's who. Up until 1908, when Britain claimed a 60-degree slice of the Antarctic pie as its own, Antarctica was the last unclaimed place on Earth, a snowy expanse where the temperature never rose above ninety degrees below zero Fahrenheit, even on the warmest of Southern days.

Free from political shenanigans and territorial claims, the penguins swam in happy and unencumbered bliss. Then, following the expeditions of Ross and Shackleton, the crown began to see Antarctica as just another piece of land to stick the Union Jack in, touching off an endless series of conflicting territorial claims by Chile, Argentina, Norway, and Australia that persist to this day.

Britain, more than any other nation, is responsible for the Industrial Revolution and its aftereffects. This includes global warming, which is gradually reducing the frozen continent to the consistency of a Slurpee. Thanks to their coal-burning ways, a good hunk of Antarctica now sits underwater, and if you ask me, that's the only piece of the great white untrammeled continent that the Evil Empire ought to get.

THEY BELIEVE
IN GOVERNMENT
THROUGH FEAR

Prehistoric natives had it pretty good. When she's not wasting all her energy filtering industrial poison out of the groundwater and coal smoke out of the air, Earth is a generous mother, providing more than enough delicious fruits, nuts, veggies, and meats to fill your local organic supermarket aisles many times over. So pardon us if we call Thomas Hobbes, godfather of Britain's political philosophy, ungrateful for characterizing life in a state of nature as "solitary, poor, nasty, brutish, and short."

Talk about seeing the empty half of the teacup. According to *Leviathan,* Hobbes's most famous work, our principal emotion is fear, and government is created not as the sum of our freedoms and aspirations but to be a giant King Kong stomping all over the country, protecting us from the monsters of famine and war that constantly torment the waking nightmare known as life. Does it get any more cynical than that?

A consummate pessimist and coward, Hobbes lived a fittingly solitary, nasty, and brutish life, though it was hardly poor or short. Hobbes's wimpy, death-fearing ways preserved him to the ripe old age of ninety-two. With no Leviathan to protect him from the uncertainties of the afterlife, he died utterly petrified of whatever was coming next.

THEY PROPAGATED THEIR CONVOLUTED SYSTEM OF MEASUREMENT AROUND THE GLOBE

The metric system is a classic example of the British imperial strategy at work. First, the Brits use their "special relationship" with the United States to settle an old score with France. Second, we fight tooth and nail on the Evil Empire's behalf for decades, in a fight we don't even have a dog in, only to receive nary a word of thanks in return.

Invented shortly after the American Revolution by the French chemist Antoine Lavoisier, the metric system (or *Système International d'Unités,* as he called it) was designed to be a universal replacement for outmoded local systems. A foot, for example, is however long the guy holding the ruler says it is. A meter, on the other hand, is equal to exactly one forty-millionth of Earth's circumference, which is equal to a metal rod kept by the French Institute. Far more efficient than the haphazard British system of measuring things in caveman units like chains, stones, poles, links, furlongs, and even hogsheads, the new, clean metric family of units distilled distance to meters, mass to grams, and volume to liters. The British switched over in 1965, but America, famously loyal even to losing causes, has had a series of false starts, publishing a new report and convening a new board every ten years or so that this time, we're finally really going to make the switch.

Until then, the old British way of measuring things continues to cost our manufacturers millions of dollars a year. The worst casualty of the metric system may have come in 1998, when the Mars Climate Orbiter burned up in the planet's atmosphere because U.S. contractor Lockheed Martin had given a key measurement in English pound-seconds instead of metric Newton-seconds. As tens of millions of U.S. tax dollars lay in shambles on the surface of the Red Planet, you could barely discern the sound of laughter coming from the graves of the old British geometers who got us hooked on their backward system in the first place.

THEY GIVE AWARDS TO COVER THEIR TRACKS

Cecil Rhodes sucked the diamonds out ㅇ which he had no deed, and committe against the native hordes that were almost geno On top of that, he was an insufferable blowhar boasting that "we" (the white English) "are the fi ...ace in the world, and the more of the world we inhabit, the better it is for the human race." He was quite open about his desire to "paint the map red," a euphemism for taking over the globe.

Yet today, we hear "Rhodes" and think of a jolly and generous philanthropist. Like many a bloated British plutocrat, Rhodes was able to erase a lifetime of imperialist bloodshed with one gesture of charity, the Rhodes Scholarship, which has since been awarded to dozens of U.S. senators, cabinet members, and Supreme Court justices, all in the name of keeping up good Anglo-American relations. But this aura of prestige and benevolence disguises Rhodes's original motive. He was interested not in furthering the education of a few bright Americans with a full-ride scholarship to Oxford so much as bringing them back into the imperial fold. "Why should we not form a secret society," he wrote, "with but one object: the furtherance of the British Empire and the bringing of the whole uncivilized world under British rule for the recovery of the United States."

While the Rhodes Foundation has thus far failed to achieve this sick dream, Rhodes's investment has paid handsome dividends in the form of thousands of American Rhodes Scholars, most of whom grew up to wield tremendous influence in American public life while nursing warm memories of their Oxford days.

THEY INVENTED
THE GIBBET

Yuck! Can it get any fouler than this? No amount of inquiry into the misdeeds of the British nation will ever get me used to the idea of the gibbet, one of most disgusting penal devices ever invented by the mind of man, a punishment so harsh that it makes crucifixion seem like getting slapped with a wet noodle.

Used in Britain up until 1832, the gibbet was an iron cage that displayed the dead body of a criminal after his hanging. It would often be hoisted up above the town square or at a prominent crossroads and remain there for as long as twenty years, so everyone could watch as the flesh putrefied and went to pieces and became food for carnivorous birds until all that remained was a skeleton. British lawmen defended these gruesome spectacles, saying they impressed the majesty of the law upon the citizenry and deterred would-be criminals.

In fact, gibbeting was an excuse for these white-wigged perverts to treat another man's body as a plaything and impose a climate of fear over their jurisdictions. And gibbeting wasn't reserved for the worst criminals—you could wind up in a gibbet for simply being aboard a pirate ship or stealing another man's sheep. You might think the British would now try to disown this part of their history, but some are actually proud of it. The town of Rye still has an old gibbet on display in its town hall. Inside is the skull of a man unlucky enough to have fallen victim to one of the most brutal practices of the Evil Empire.

THEY COULDN'T STAND UP TO NAPOLEON

Few figures in history annoy me more than Napoleon, yet another starry-eyed European who'd read too many books and believed it was his personal destiny to take over the world. Napoleon was more successful than most, waging an inspired, if deluded, fifteen-year series of military campaigns against the Italians, Germans, and Russians; taking over some big chunks of Africa; and crowning himself Emperor Napoleon I.

I will readily admit that it was a British general, the Duke of Wellington, who eventually put a halt to Napoleon's ever-widening ambitions at the Battle of Waterloo, but the British sure took their sweet time deciding to move against him. Only when Napoleon started leering at India, the brightest jewel in the Evil Empire's crown, did Britain finally act. In the meantime, Napoleon was left to tromp all over the European continent unmolested for a full two years.

While I do give credit to the courageous Wellington for Napoleon's defeat, along with the skilled naval maneuvering of the dashing and diamond-hatted Lord Nelson, Britain ultimately must thank the deadly cold of the Russian winter for her freedom. Had half a million Frenchmen not perished on Napoleon's foolish march to Moscow, Westminster would likely have become yet another provincial capital of the glorious French Republic.

THEY BEFOULED THE WORLD'S STAGES WITH INCOMPREHENSIBLE DRAMAS

Despite the major cleavage that tends to bunch up at the top of those lacy Victorian corsets, the plays of William Shakespeare are way overrated. Professors like him because he kept so many dead words alive, which gives them something to talk about. Actors like him because his roles let them inhabit their true selves—vainglorious, overly solemn nitwits who speak as though they've got tubas lodged in their throats. But the common man doesn't like William Shakespeare, because even for native speakers of English, his plays are too damn hard to understand.

Good stories should be like a gangster movie: accessible, excessively violent, and easy to understand. You shouldn't have to whip out a concordance to figure out what the hell the people on the stage are talking about. Also, good stories should be about everyday people, and most of Shakespeare's characters are royals of one stripe or another. The sum effect is to make theater yet another pretentious token of "culture," a way to show off that you went to such-and-such private school and spend your evenings reading the *Oxford English Dictionary* by candlelight. Please. We'll take Tarantino any day of the week.

THEY POLLUTED SINCERE, FREETHINKING DISCOURSE WITH SARCASM, IRONY, AND OTHER FORMS OF PERNICIOUS WIT

A wit is someone who sits around and talks but actually does next to nothing. Try to prod him into getting up off his ass, and he'll twist your words into a cruel pun and use them against you. For instance, when a fellow member of Parliament told eighteenth-century politician John Wilkes that "You, sir, will either die of the pox or the gallows," Wilkes responded, "That would depend on whether I embrace your lordship's mistresses or your principles." Helpless before the powers of common sense, the Englishman must resort to flippant sophistries to save face.

In America, you can lose your job and your marriage through such behavior. In Britain, they'll give you a medal for it. Even the brilliant careers of Oscar Wilde and Sir Winston Churchill were accorded no real respect until some random comeback they tossed off in the pub one night finally made it into *Quincy Whitechapel's Book of Quotations* or *Her Majesty's Royal Compendium of Silly Anecdotes.* These verbal jabs may seem like harmless fun, but in fact British humor is a vicious imperial strategy designed to reinforce the established pecking order and gently disarm any would-be rebellions before they gather any steam.

THEY NEVER GOT OVER THE WAR OF 1812

The English never got over 1776. Like an abusive ex-boyfriend after a bad breakup, Britain was rabid with heartbroken anger and wanted to give us a beatdown as soon as possible. He just couldn't tolerate all the fun we were having—the cozy alliances we were building with snazzily dressed Frenchmen, the fact that we no longer needed a jealous old king's permission to explore hot new freedoms and wild frontiers. The ink on the treaty that ended the War of Independence was hardly dry when the Brits started breaking it, refusing to give up their forts, stopping our sovereign ships on the high seas, and encouraging the Indians to fight against us. Who can blame them? Any wannabe global power would be bitter about losing their toehold on the richest continent in the world. America was so damn hot that John Bull couldn't bring himself to let go.

Now remembered as a footnote, the War of 1812 was deadly serious. The Evil Empire's army torched Washington, D.C. You read right: The British burned our capital to the ground right after we built it. It was by the red glare of the rockets they fired on us that "The Star-Spangled Banner" was written. Not exactly gentlemanly behavior.

Of all the courageous American volunteer soldiers who left farm and family behind to participate in the conflict, perhaps none were of harder core than the fighting Vermonters, who sang, "If you rule all our land, you'll rule all our graves." Needless to say, John Bull was sent whimpering back across the Atlantic for a second time, his imperial hard-on dangling limply between his legs.

THEIR ARCHEOLOGISTS PANDER TO AND DEFRAUD THE PUBLIC

In 1912, the Evil Empire was reeling. Confronted with the scientific fact that human life began in Africa, they felt threatened and ashamed of the thousands of years they'd spent dancing around bonfires and wearing animal skins. They needed their own claim to grand ancient origins. Enter the Piltdown Man, whose skull was discovered in a Sussex gravel pit. With the big-brained skull of a man and the elongated jaw of an ape, Piltdown Man was proof that ancient Englishmen (despite their aversion to building, writing, and washing) were as precocious as their cutlass-swinging Ottoman counterparts.

Too bad Piltdown Man wasn't real. Turns out some anonymous prankster had taken a chimpanzee jaw, broken off the ends, and attached it to the skull of a man from the Middle Ages, which he'd chemically aged to appear thousands of years older than it actually was. Piltdown Man wound up making the case not that early Brits had especially large brains, but that modern Brits have small and gullible ones.

THEY WORSHIPED
THE ROMANS

The early English were a savage people. They lived in caves and indulged in human, and sometimes animal, sacrifices. We know very little about them because they did not see fit to write anything down. The first time they appear in recorded history is as a captive people in the diaries of Gaius Julius Caesar, who watched with glee as his disciplined legions made short work of wretched spear-carrying English and Celtic tribes.

The four centuries that England would spend under Roman occupation drove home the lesson of just how painful it is to be on the receiving end of a more advanced civilization's world-conquering ambitions. These years of subjugation made a deep impression on the English psyche. It was the Romans, not the British, who first established London as a center of trade and decision-making and who built the first bridge there, across the Thames. Knowing how intensely his country-men yearned to get out from under Rome's shadow, the talented British historian William Gibbon chose to make his career with the *Decline and Fall of the Roman Empire* at the end of the eighteenth century, just as Britain was licking its lips, realizing the new powers of its navy, and counting down the days until history would acknowledge it as a lat-ter-day Rome.

THEY INVENTED
CHILD LABOR

Beginning in the late 1700s, poor and lower-middle class British parents looked to their children not as treasures that needed to be coddled and nurtured but doe-eyed money machines who were expected to pull their own weight within the family. They sent them out into factories and even mines, where they would often work for longer hours and lower wages than their adult counterparts. Many suffered from permanent disabilities after being compelled by their bosses to crawl through narrow mine shafts and maintain large, powerful cotton gins.

In 1788, two out of every three workers employed by Britain's textile industry was a child. To get an idea of just how bad the situation was, consider the Factory Acts, a series of reforms passed by Parliament in response to public outcry. The first of these acts, in 1802, mandated that children could work no more than twelve hours a day and sleep no more than two to a bed. It wasn't until 1833 that the workday for children as young as nine was reduced to nine hours, and accidental deaths on the job went widely unreported until 1844. If this is how Britain treated her own children, imagine what the colonies had to put up with!

THEY PERFECTED AND SPREAD THE TEDIUM OF FACTORY LIFE

For the last hundred years, the life of modern man has been built on a routine of waking up, eating breakfast, washing, getting dressed, and trading away the next nine hours of drudgery for a monthly paycheck. This is what we call "work," and it, like so many other dreary things, is a British invention.

Nowadays work has meaning and variety, of course, but old-school work of the repetitive, meatpacking, assembly-line sort began in Birmingham, with Matthew Boulton's Soho Factory. Established in 1761, it turned metal into buttons, buckles, and coins and turned the men that made these commodities into mindless robots. Boulton used the profits from this venture to live in high style at Soho House, where he entertained himself by discussing philosophy, politics, and science with the leading minds of his day. Meanwhile, his workers drowned the deadening effects of their workday into pint after pint of frothy mead.

To be fair, Boulton was kind enough to make sure his factory was clean and safe by eighteenth-century standards, but the industrialists who would propagate his factory model over the next two hundred years had no such scruples. By consuming the greater share of the workingman's energies while dulling his mind with repetition, it didn't take much to manipulate his political sensibilities. In this way, industrialists could fill the ranks of Parliament with cronies who would send British fighting ships overseas under the Union Jack and secure new materials and markets to keep the factories humming.

THEY INVENTED
SLUMS

For all the tons of gold, silver, and raw material flowing into Britain over the course of the nineteenth century, you might think that nary an Englishman would go hungry, especially those living in the city of London. And you would be wrong. The moment factory owners and aristocrats stepped inside their palatial country homes and leather-chaired club rooms, they forgot about the plight of the working men and women, the folks who swept their chimneys, scrubbed their teacups, and generally made their life of luxury possible. Of these, the luckiest butlers, footmen, and maids dwelt in cramped servant quarters, usually located in the basement of their lord's manor. These were far from ideal, but they did provide a guarantee of a heated room and adequate food and water for survival.

Less fortunate were the slum dwellers, who lived in London's sprawling shantytowns without the benefit of heat or even running water. Rivers of sewage coursed down the middle of narrow alleyways, where mothers were forced to turn to prostitution and orphan children begged for pennies in the streets. Most, as they grew older, would realize a life of thievery was the only way out of dying a pauper. The polished chrome of gin and beer halls was the only relief from the squalor, and as of 1880 London was home to literally hundreds of thousands of destitute alcoholics. The wealthier the Evil Empire grew, the more its arrogant engineers were able to ignore its victims, even those on Britain's own shores.

THEY ENCOURAGED
AND SUBSIDIZED
THE SLAVE TRADE

While modern Britain likes to look down its collective nose at America's history of slavery and segregation, the British themselves were avid slave traders, putting some three million Africans into chains between 1640 and 1807. It was British slavers who first devised the notoriously cruel "middle passage," where men were packed head to toe like cargo for the Atlantic Crossing. The practice was sanctioned by Queen Elizabeth I herself, who specifically authorized privateers—professional, state-sanctioned pirates—to capture and sell free Africans, so long as they kicked back a portion of the proceeds to finance her nascent imperial dreams.

It was British taskmasters who first taught Southern planters how to wield the whip, and British captains whose Liverpool and Birmingham ships brought their scandalous cargoes up for auction at Charleston and Richmond. As the Evil Empire gobbled up Africa, slavers saw yet another chance to force slaves to work the soil. They lived an existence of such barren poverty that even Mark Twain, a seasoned Southerner, was moved to write: "This is slavery, and is several times worse than the American slavery which used to pain England so much; for when this Rhodesian slave is sick . . . he must support himself or starve—his master is under no obligation to support him." So get off your high horse, England. Back in the day you did your share of slaving.

THEY'RE A BEACON OF PRUDERY AND SNOBBERY

It is a truth universally acknowledged that the people of Regency England—and the novels of Jane Austen—were a flock of hidebound bores who managed to turn every social situation into an elaborate performance of rank and protocol, and who devoted their lives to snuffing out spontaneous fun wherever it arose. London pedestrians in the 1840s and '50s moved with clockwork precision, guided by hundreds of invisible rules that dictated when to bow, whom to say hello to, under what circumstances a gentleman should offer a lady his arm, etc. The women were trapped inside cocoons of corsets and expectations for constantly submissive "ladylike" behavior. They would spend a decade building a reputation for modesty and lose it in a day by wearing a dress that showed half an inch of bare ankle.

Castrated by all this invasive etiquette, the men compensated by exaggerating their height with starched collars and tall, phallic hats. Rules for dining and polite conversation kept everyone's focus off the plight of England's working poor and on which fork to use for the next course. Granted, this was more than a century ago, but today's Britain still abounds with high-handed industrialists, stone-faced women, and servile bellhops who stammer and grovel for the honor of carrying your highness's baggage.

In a truly free society, respect is due to every man and woman; in Britain it is still carefully divvied up according to a silent Victorian code.

THEY LOVE A
GOOD HANGING

Every society has a spectacle at its center. Here in America, we have the Super Bowl. France has the world's grandest bicycle race. North Korea, even, has its Mass Games, where squads of terrified citizens march around stadiums in formation, like robots.

For hundreds of years, the public sport that Britain organized itself around was hanging. Up until the nineteenth century, the English had more than two hundred excuses to string up their fellow men. You could be hanged for sodomy, fraud, and theft. Even spending too much time with gypsies could win you a date with the gallows. In many small towns, hangings were greeted as enthusiastically as parades. Parents would pack a picnic lunch and bring their children along to watch. Visiting lords would watch the ritualized killings through opera glasses while sipping sweet port on their hosts' balconies. "Lunch and a hanging" was the rough equivalent of "dinner and a movie," a generic and widely accepted formula for a wholesome first date. Executions were instructional, renewing the slavish feelings of fear and awe that keep British society running, as well as saving a bit of money on keeping the inmate population housed and fed.

Perhaps British civilization was fond of hangings because it reminded them of even less humane days, when drawing and quartering and even beheading by ax were the norm. "A mere hanging," you can almost imagine them saying to their youngsters as they wait for the convicted to die. "In my day we weren't so soft on crime." Hangings continued to be carried out in public until 1868, when at long last the immortal souls of Britain's convicts started being passed up to their maker in the privacy of their cells.

THEY INVENTED THE
VELVET ROPE

MEMBERS ONLY

From VIP-only discotheques to the Groucho Club to the House of Lords to the royal family itself, the British get off on having a crowd of commoners massed at the door, begging to be let into the party. They like it even more when the system for separating who's included and who's excluded is nakedly unfair, and the walls separating the inside from the outside have lots of windows so the poor losers on the outside can see what they're missing.

It takes snobbery as naked as this to give birth to a movement as angry and democratic as punk, formed by a nation of working-class misfits so sure they'd be rejected by Britain's staid and selective value system that they decided to flip the whole system the bird before it got the chance to do the same to them.

Really, the Evil Empire's snobby reach never stopped shrinking. The revolutionary rejection of the royal hierarchy started with Tom Paine and Paul Revere in the eighteenth century and continued with Shaka Zulu and Mahatma Gandhi in the nineteenth and into the twentieth. Even after the Evil Empire was lost, the power of snobbery continued to wane on its own turf, as Sid Vicious and Mick Farren gave an entire generation of British youths alternatives to their parents' tweedy and traditional lives.

THEY SUPPORTED THE CONFEDERACY

No event in American history reveals more about the essence of the British character than the American Civil War. On one side was the Union, antislavery industrialists who were the legitimate heirs of U.S. sovereignty. On the other side were the Confederates, a fragile aristocracy of planter gentry held up by masses of black slaves and red-necked whipcrackers. Who do you think the British supported? Drawn in by the romance of cotillions and duels, the brazen sense of racial superiority, intriguingly similar flag designs, and the need to keep Virginia cotton flowing into Liverpool mills, the Evil Empire naturally sympathized with the Confederates.

The Brits had been blowing kisses to Jefferson Davis and his treasonous band for a few months when Davis sent his henchman James Mason as a diplomat to London aboard the San Jacinto, a steamship carrying the Royal Mail. A Union captain stopped the traitorous vessel just off the coast of Cuba and hauled Mason back to Boston to stand trial. Rather than give up their little gambit, the British government demanded that Mason be freed—as though he were the emissary of a real country!

After much vain blustering on both sides, President Abraham Lincoln proved the bigger man and let Mason continue on to London, where he failed to convince Parliament to back the Confederates. Good choice. Whatever the Union might have thought of the Brits, there wasn't enough hate to want to mop the floor with them for yet a third time.

THEY INVENTED THE MACHINE GUN

By 1889, most of the bravest men in the Evil Empire had long left their homeland, either to seek their fortunes in the new colonies or to lay down their lives on foreign shores in service of the crown. The army and navy were left with the country's most timid stock— cowardly lifers who stood little chance against the elite cavalrymen of Prussia or the mighty Zulu warriors of Zimbabwe.

But just when Britain's fighting heart began to flounder, her propensity for devising ever more deadly killing devices came through in the form of the machine gun. Invented and named for Sir Hiram Maxim, the Maxim gun could fire five hundred rounds a minute, giving teams of five men the firepower of one hundred muskets. Known as the Devil's Paintbrush for its ability to sweep the field clean with one pivot of its howling muzzle, the Maxim gun marked a turning point in the history of modern warfare. No longer was war a gentleman's game, with staged battles guided by the laws of chivalry. Now it was a mad rush to see who could pile the enemy bodies up higher and faster. This terrified the British ranks, who calmed themselves by singing this gruesome lullaby:

> *Whatever happens, we have got*
> *The Maxim gun, and they have not.*

THEY GERMINATED JINGOISM

Anyone who's been close to war hates it with a passion. But when you have a nation of prideful but frightened Englishmen who can send a nation of hardened Irishmen out to fight their battles for them, then read all about the glorious result in the day's papers, you get jingoism, a civilian population's unstudied love of war. The Evil Empire was the first country with an army sufficiently professional and separated from the mainstream population to experience jingoism. The term comes from Britain, specifically this song:

> *We don't want to fight*
> *But, by Jingo, if we do,*
> *We've got the ships,*
> *We've got the men,*
> *We've got the money, too.*

First sung in the streets by a fevered mob in 1876, this little ditty demonstrates how the Englishman uses his country's military engagements as a distraction from the frustrations and anxieties he has about his own daily life.

Shockingly, the song continued to appear among working-class warmongers as late as the 1982 Falklands war, when Britain, having buried two generations of her men in two World Wars, ought to have known better than to cavalierly strut to the other side of the hemisphere looking for trouble. It just goes to show you that no amount of bloodshed can stop a cocksure Englishman's sense of his own inherent superiority from overruling his conscience. And all too often our own armies are dragged into battle behind him.

THEY FILLED THEIR MUSEUMS WITH STOLEN TREASURES

The British Museum in London is little more than a pirate's trophy case, showing off the results of various cultural rapes that red-coated lackeys perpetuated on ancient sites around the world. One of the most egregious thefts is the Parthenon marbles, taken from Greece in 1816 by Earl Thomas Bruce, who had them chopped off the oldest and greatest temple known to Western civilization, hacked to pieces, and shipped to his estate in England. After handing these treasures over to the British Museum, so-called conservators caused them further irreversible damage by scrubbing and scouring them, stripping away their natural, protective coating until they were as pale and vulnerable to the elements as the skin of a Welsh washerwoman.

Robert Anderson, director of the British Museum, has refused to return the marbles to their rightful place in Greece, or even lend them to the city of Athens for a brief tour. In his words:

> *Today's national boundaries and cultural mixes bear little relation to the ancient past. The restitutionist premise, that whatever was made in a country must return to an original geographical site, would empty both the British Museum and the other great museums of the world.*

Sure. By that logic, I could burgle Buckingham Palace, steal Queen Elizabeth's crown jewels, keep them under armed guard in my basement, and then charge all comers ten bucks a head for a look.

THEY GUNNED DOWN
TENS OF THOUSANDS OF
DEFENSELESS AFRICANS

On a desolate African plain in 1884, eight thousand British infantrymen carrying high-powered machine guns and rifles met a horde of Ottoman soldiers armed with nothing more than spears and a few old muskets. When the smoke cleared, ten thousand Ottomans were dead and fifteen thousand were wounded, most of them killed by lightning streams of belt-fed bullets from the Brits' Maxim machine guns.

The British, meanwhile, lost fewer than fifty men. Yet these ridiculously uneven ratios failed to arouse the Brits' famous sense of fair play. A young Winston Churchill even celebrated the "Battle" of Omdurman in breathlessly bloodthirsty prose:

> *What enterprise that an enlightened community may attempt is more noble and profitable than the reclamation from barbarism of a fertile region and large populations?… The act is virtuous, the exercise invigorating, and the result often extremely profitable.*

He neglects to mention the barbaric killings that his enlightened nation performed on anyone who felt otherwise.

THEY INVENTED THE CONCENTRATION CAMP

British historians would have you believe that it was the Nazis who constructed the first concentration camps. While those goosestepping creeps were the first to use gas chambers and ovens to accomplish their genocidal goals, the term *concentration camp* was actually coined half a century before, to describe the awful refugee tent cities that Britain sent Boer and black African captives to during the Boer Wars in South Africa.

With little food and water, conditions in the camps were so terrible that 30 percent of the occupants died, mostly women and young children. One particularly horrifying story puts a British officer's club near the entrance of one of the camps. When the club's pine floorboards wore out, the stingy British colonials sold them for a shilling each so the Boer mothers could build makeshift coffins for their dead little ones.

Instead of being ashamed of this episode in their imperial history, the British actually commemorate it to this day, with many British soccer teams calling areas of their grandstands Spion Kop, to honor one of the Boer Wars' goriest battles.

THEY GAVE KARL MARX
HIS FIRST JOB

Wherever Karl Marx went, the authorities knew the bearded young philosopher would stir up trouble. At school in Germany, the professors feared the teachings of young Marx's coterie. Over the next decade or so, Marx's politics got him expelled from no fewer than three European countries—France, Germany, and Belgium—before finally nestling into the welcoming bosom of Britain, the one European nation foolish enough to allow him to stay, where he would spend the rest of his life. *Capital,* his life's work, advocates abolishing investment and private property and handing over control of production to an all-powerful government.

What could inspire such madness? Living in London, that's what. A work that contains as much straight journalism as philosophy, *Capital* shows us that Marx was moved to concoct his harebrained revolutionary schemes due to the horrors he witnessed in London's nineteenth-century factories, where workers had virtually no rights and were exploited by their bosses every day. Had he only chosen the open prairies of, say, Montana as a surrogate home, he might never have been moved to write the poison that gave birth to the Soviet Union and brought about the deaths of more than twenty million at the hands of Josef Stalin. And now we've got yet another red menace, China, to deal with.

Thanks a lot, Marx. And thank you, London, for giving Marx a warm bed, four squares, and so much inspiration.

THEY MOLD YOUNG MEN INTO MINDLESS TWITS WITH THE BOY SCOUTS

In America, your early years are a glorious time of freedom and experimentation. You take a few wild rolls in the hay, light your toys on fire, and do one or two things that could have earned you some jail time if you'd waited for your adult years to get into them. See Tom Sawyer and Huckleberry Finn, two kids who knew how to be kids.

Jealous of kids' naturally free-spirited ways, the stuffy British aristocrat Robert Baden-Powell founded the Boy Scouts in 1907. The organization's supposed purpose was to teach budding imperialists valuable lessons of independence and self reliance, but in practice this took the form of wrapping them in starched uniforms and having them march back and forth like brownshirted fascists. Badges were then awarded to whoever best followed the bellowing drill master's instructions.

American scouting began in 1910, but really took off after World War II, when the Soviet threat and postwar conformity made afterschool military training seem like an appropriate child-rearing technique. Scouting wasn't all bad—it helped many children of the '30s like Neil Armstrong and Donald Rumsfeld avoid falling into hippie-dippie baby boomer lassitude, but think what might have been achieved if the minds of our boys hadn't been swaddled in imperialist khaki.

THEY MADE NICE WITH HITLER

Totalitarian dictators like Adolf Hitler don't appear out of thin air. Their rise to power occurs gradually, on the front page of each day's paper. Each generation faces at least one of these armed madmen, who snack on small countries and wash them down with the blood of the racially impure. When that time comes, the leaders of the free world are given a choice: Either nip the bastards in the bud or barricade the door, bury your head beneath a pillow, and pray that the bully tires himself out rampaging around the neighborhood.

In the late 1930s, Prime Minister Neville Chamberlain did what many a British man has done when faced with a brute who doesn't respect the rules of etiquette. He lost his nerve. Chamberlain stood aside while German tanks rolled through Austria and Czechoslovakia. He treated Hitler like a gentleman and fellow statesman, inviting him to diplomatic tours and dinners. They went for walks together and posed for photographs. In 1938, even as Nazi officials began vandalizing synagogues and rounding up Jews, Chamberlain boasted that he'd obtained "peace in our time" by flying to Germany and getting Hitler's signature on a piece of paper. The crowds that greeted him at the airport roared with delight.

Today, we're fortunate enough that Mssrs. Bush the Elder and Bush the Younger took the bud-nipping approach with Saddam Hussein. Yet another instance of Americans doing whatever it takes to protect the world's freedom while wishy-washy British statesmen wring their hands and whine about what's to be done.

D-DAY. DID THEY DO THEIR SHARE?

June 6, 1944. All Western Civilization was on the line. The Nazi fiends had cornered the freedom-loving Allies, who were now forced to stake everything on an all-or-nothing gamble to establish a beachhead on the French coast. Everyone involved knew that D-Day's success or failure would determine the course of world history for centuries to come. Over a few months, the Allies drove the pestilence of totalitarianism from the globe. Mussolini was hanged and dismembered by the furious Italian masses. Hitler, that pencil-necked coward, blew his brains out in his underground bunker.

But on the beaches of D-Day, the operation that sent World War II into triple overtime, American corpses outnumbered the Brits 2 to 1. U.S. forces had 6,603 casualties, British forces 2,700, and even the famously pusillanimous Canadians had nearly one thousand. You would think that the sons of Britain, having endured the Blitz and fighting for their homeland's very survival, would have been the first to put themselves in harm's way. Yet somehow we wound up absorbing the brunt of the German counterattack, while Britain assumed a posture that would become familiar to it over the ensuing decades—the sidekick.

THEY'RE DESCENDED FROM CANNIBALS

The real story of ancient Britain is told not by the Piltdown Man fraud but the gnawed, marrowless bones of Cheddar Man, discovered in a cave in Somerset. Born around 7000 BC, Cheddar Man's bones were covered with grooves from knives and—ugh!—teeth. Poor Cheddar Man! His countrymen had sucked the sweet, juicy marrow out of his bones. Cheddar Man, it seems, was killed in his youth and then eaten by a wild pack of British cannibals. To many ancient peoples (who British ethnographers would later deride as "primitive"), these years were the golden age of progress and enlightenment. To the Brits, it was the Stone Age, enshrouded in the darkness of animal worship, ritual sacrifice, and, as the fate of poor Cheddar Man suggests, men chasing around and snacking on their comrades.

The magnificent edifice of British science, naturally, tried to distance itself from Cheddar Man, hypothesizing that the British were descended not from cannibals but wandering farmers who had replaced the hunters who made Cheddar Man into a meal. This theory, as comforting as it was to the nation's pride, was quickly refuted when the DNA from three residents of today's village of Cheddar were found to have a close match for the Cheddar skeleton's DNA. One of them, a schoolteacher, lived just a half mile from the cave where Cheddar Man was found, showing that the bluest of British blood may have once coursed through the blackest of cannibal hearts.

THE DEVISED AND PROPAGATED THE THEORY OF THE WELFARE STATE

The U.S. government is currently more than $12 trillion in debt. We were talked into taking on these massive obligations by the eccentric theories of John Maynard Keynes, who proposed that government ought to do more than keep the lights turned on and the army at the ready. They were also to be the employer of last resort, spending copiously on public projects and hiring the unemployed to shelter us during any economic downturn.

Franklin Delano Roosevelt put these theories to excellent use, carrying us through the Great Depression. He had the unemployed rake leaves, build roads, write the histories of their home cities; anything to keep the men leaving the house every day and new paychecks flowing into the national economy.

But all this governmental intervention had one very harmful Keynesian side effect: the false belief that every able-bodied person, no matter how unskilled his mind, unwashed his body, or stubborn his character, deserves to have a full-time, well-paid job by dint of having been born in this country, a belief that persists today. Thanks to Keynesian economics, foundry workers, typewriter mechanics, travel agents, and other displaced workers sit around the house waiting for the government to bail them out when they ought to be hitting the books and then the streets to find new jobs. With Chinese laborers churning out product for pennies an hour, we need to abolish Keynesian slackerdom once and for all.

THEY GLORIFY COKEHEADS

How can America be expected to fight the war on drugs when depraved British novelists like Sir Arthur Conan Doyle cranked out potboiler after potboiler about a heroic detective, Sherlock Holmes, who toots a quick a line of cocaine up his nose whenever he's bored? You read that right: Sherlock Holmes was a cokehead, and not an infrequent one either. We see him in the Doyle stories snorting the white stuff and shooting morphine into his arm whenever the trail goes cold, so we can only imagine how often he was on junk in between the stories, when there wasn't a case.

His roommate Watson knew how bad Holmes's problem was. "For years," he mused, "I had gradually weaned him from that drug mania which had threatened once to check his remarkable career. Now I knew that under ordinary conditions he no longer craved for this artificial stimulus, but I was well aware that the fiend was not dead . . ." Does Doyle really expect us to believe that periodical snowstorms of raw dopamine wouldn't dull the sharpest deductive mind in London? It certainly may have eroded his libido—Holmes never appears interested in any women and is sometimes witnessed in a fit of frustration, unloading his revolver into the apartment wall and completely freaking his poor bachelor roommate out of his wits.

We can only conclude that Doyle intended Holmes to be a twisted parody of Victorian manhood—rational and law-abiding in public while enslaved to his impulses in the confines of his home.

THEY CAUSED THE GREAT DEPRESSION

E ver since we stopped crawling around on all fours like baboons, man has lusted for gold. Gold's heaviness, shininess, and scarcity made it the perfect way to store and transfer value. And so before we even knew what money was, gold was the coin of the land. For centuries, you could march on down to the central bank with a wheelbarrow full of any of the world's major paper currencies—U.S. dollars, Swiss francs, Spanish pesetas, whatever—and receive actual physical gold in return.

All that came to a halt with World War I. The Evil Empire (the leading global power of the time) went deep into debt to finance its campaign against Germany. The plan was to go off the gold standard, print millions of pounds sterling to buy American ships, kick the crap out of the Germans, and then force them to pay massive reparations to cover the war tab. But rather than a stern bulldog of fiscal responsibility, Britain proved to be more like a teenage girl shopping at Harrod's with Uncle Sam's credit card. President Calvin Coolige tried to talk her out of it, but Winston Churchill, Chancellor of the Exchequer at the time, desperately needed more paper money to finance his war toys. With a wave of Winston's hand, the global gold standard was gone, and the world's money was transformed from a certificate promising an ancient metal into pretty pieces of scrip. Except for six years of sanity in the '20s, Britain never went back on the gold standard.

The rest of the world was soon forced to follow. With Germany broke and angry, and money transformed by British profligacy into meaningless paper, the entire global economy soon collapsed, and the world was plunged into the long nightmare of the Depression and World War II.

THEY HAVE A FASCIST, NAZI-LOVING MEAN STREAK

We all know the stories of how the British joined the rest of the Allies to fight fascism abroad in the second World War. But few acknowledge the prominent role fascists, racists, and nationalists have played in Britain's domestic scene, part of the natural outgrowth of a century of imperialist propaganda that told generations of kids in subtle and not-so-subtle ways that simply because they'd been born on the British Isles, they were a superior species of humanity.

In the years leading up to World War II, Sir Oswald Mosley, a British Member of Parliament, stirred these pots of racist foment by meeting with Mussolini and forming the British Union of Fascists, who donned black shirts and marched in the streets. While the United States had similar movements, they more or less died with World War II. The remnants of British fascism, on the other hand, have survived to the present day, in the form of the xenophobic New National Front, now known as the British National Party, which openly declares that it exists "for the preservation of the national and ethnic character of the British people. . . . [The BNP] is wholly opposed to any form of racial integration between British and non-European peoples." Imagine if the American Ku Klux Klan ran candidates for office! Well, the BNP is still popular enough to hold 53 seats on local municipal councils.

Still sore about having lost vast tracts of their Evil Empire, the country's fascist streak hangs onto the idea of their genetic superiority.

THEY HUNG OUT AND
HAD BEERS WITH THEIR
GOOD PAL MUSSOLINI

As I've discussed, Neville Chamberlain failed to recognize the threat posed by Adolf Hitler. Chamberlain traveled with Hitler, dined with Hitler, and, after the invasion of Czechoslovakia, did not even realize that a treaty signed by Hitler wasn't worth the paper it was printed on. But if Britain's leaders were soft on Hitler in his early career, they went even easier on schoolteacher-gone-wild Benito Mussolini, who sometimes showed off his affinity for Westminster styles by donning a bowler hat, the traditional uniform of the buttoned-up English gentleman.

Imperial England and Imperial Italy under Il Duce had a few things in common. Both had fought against Germany and Austria in World War I. Both worshiped the romantic memory of Caesar's Rome—British aristocrats were often memorialized in marble in centurion garb, and Mussolini named his fascist party after the *fasces,* rods, of Roman law. Impressed by Mussolini's iron hand, Winston Churchill hailed him as "the Roman Genius . . . the greatest lawgiver among living men." British Prime Minster Lloyd George intoned "either the world decides to follow Mussolini, or the world is doomed." Only when Mussolini tried to seize an empire of his own by attacking Ethiopia did Britain finally turn against him. Even then, the decision was based not on distaste for the fascist project but the imperial desire to keep Africa for themselves.

THEY PERFECTED THE ART
OF CARPET BOMBING

O f the many ways man has devised to murder his fellow man by the thousands, bombing ranks right up there with firing squads and gas chambers in terms of brutality, effectiveness, and embodiment of pure evil. British revisionist historians would have you believe that only Germany under Hitler and Russia under Stalin engaged in such atrocities, when in fact the British mercilessly carpet-bombed civilian German populations.

This was more than "total war," more than an attempt to sap the German national will or throw a cog into the gears of her war machine. This was retaliation, pure and simple—bloodthirsty vengeance for the London blitz. British bombers dropping four thousand tons of explosives killed somewhere between 25,000 and 140,000 residents of Dresden, leaving the city's center a blackened, smoking hole. Four out of every five buildings in the entire city were damaged or destroyed. Even an editor from the *London Times* called it a war crime.

If carpet bombing and civilian casualties were necessary to bring the war to a quick end and ultimately preserve human life, why couldn't Churchill spare a single bomber to disrupt the flow of Jewish refugees to the death camps of Auschwitz and Bergen-Belsen? He was likely sore that Germany's bombers had forced him to move his plush ministerial offices to a basement beneath ten feet of concrete.

THEY BRAINWASH THEIR PEOPLE WITH STATE-FUNDED MEDIA

I relish the diversity of views brought to my eyes and ears by the free-market media system of the United States. If I want sprightly, right-wing commentary on the day's events, I turn on Rupert Murdoch's Fox News. If I'm in the mood for something more left wing, I tune into Jon Stewart's *The Daily Show*. Or if I want things played right down the middle, I trust CNN to give it to me straight. By sifting through this bouquet of colorful perspectives, the American people are able to make informed choices about what's true and what's garbage.

When it comes to television, the British, on the other hand, are at the mercy of a single overbearing news provider. Rather than reveling in free speech and proud independence, the BBC must please the powerful interests of the Queen and her ministers. Responsible for two television stations, five radio networks, and the vast majority of broadcast influence in the UK, the BBC continually receives subtle and not-so-subtle threats from Parliament whenever it deviates too far from the national agenda, to either appoint their political cronies to the BBC's board of governors or deprive it of precious funds by raising its licensing fees.

These days, BBC World can be heard parroting Tony Blair's ambivalent feelings about the war on terror to American audiences through its simpering sister, NPR.

THEY'RE WAY
TOO POLITE

Americans aren't "conversationalists." We don't talk for the sake of amusement, we talk to get things done, and we say what we mean. Like the French, we're polite up to a point, knowing how to disagree without being disagreeable, which, Michael Moore and Anne Coulter notwithstanding, is at the heart of healthy civic debate. The British, on the other hand, are scared to death of coming across as insincere, blustery, or the slightest bit offensive. Trained to conceal their actual opinions since birth, they come across like Mr. Bean, a jumbled mess of mannered reactions, stock formulas, and misapplied rules from moldy etiquette books. Their graces are so stilted and studied, the schoolmaster's paddle seems to have whipped any natural, innocent charms out of them long ago.

This is bad for interesting dinner party conversation but even worse for literature and philosophy. Ever since we started keeping track of such things during the Enlightenment, the British have lagged far behind their French and German counterparts in producing thinkers of the first class. The Germans have their Nietzsche, Goethe, and Hegel. The French have Voltaire, Sartre, and Rousseau. The British have . . . who? Lord Byron? Francis Bacon?

Good, sure, but not great. The Germans have *Faust*. The English have *Alice in Wonderland*. Ashamed of their shoddy record in the world-class brains department, the Brits have had to import genius from around the world and claim it as their own. The Poets' Corner at Westminster Abbey is filled with Anglo-friendly Americans (ringers!) like Henry James and T. S. Eliot, who were suckered into expatriating to artificially boost England's collective IQ.

THEIR POLITICIANS ARE SO DEBAUCHED THEY MAKE CLINTON LOOK LIKE A CHOIRBOY

The puritanical U.S. media has us believing that our politicians are a bunch of lecherous old men who consider marriage a covenant of convenience and can't help but paw whatever cute piece of ass floats by. But whatever dicking around our electeds may have done is positively G-rated compared with the Brits. At least two Prime Ministers—Lloyd George and John Major—have kept mistresses while in office. The current Deputy Prime Minister, John Prescott, was so brazen about his affair with his secretary that he's said to have whipped out his majesty's pale warship in his office. Topping the list of official perverts is M.P. Stephen Milligan, whose corpse was found bound and gagged, naked except for ladies' stockings and a pair of suspenders. Alone and clad in this bondage gear, he had died as a result of autoerotic asphyxiation, the attempt to intensify one's orgasm by cutting off the flow of air through the windpipe. Now *that* is a dirty political sex scandal the likes of which we've never seen on this side of the Atlantic.

THEY SECRETLY DREAM OF RECOVERING THEIR LOST EMPIRE

They say radical Islam has a long memory, counting time in centuries, not decades, mischievously rubbing its hands and waiting for the moment when we can return to the good old days of sultans, sheiks, and strict Koranic law. We shouldn't blame them. The memory of empire—even an evil empire—can be so alluring to ambitious nationalists that it can survive for lifetimes, even centuries. The sound of an imperial heart beating inside British chests could last be heard during the squabble over the Falkland Islands, a group of tiny islands off the coast of South America that are one of Britain's last colonial possessions.

In 1982, Argentina tried to distract her citizens from their poor, politically repressed existence by trying to pry the Falklands away from Britain's dying imperial grasp. For the Royal Air Force and Navy, this skirmish would prove a sort of last hurrah. Britain sent cutting-edge fighter jets and aircraft carriers to beat back the Argentine's underwhelming forces, and Prime Minister Margaret Thatcher is said to have even considered deploying a nuclear strike against Argentina if things didn't go the British way.

Fortunately, the Brits did manage to recover their islands and a small scrap of lost pride. President Ronald Reagan, who had his hands full beating back yet another Evil Empire—the Soviet Union—wondered aloud why the Iron Lady was making such a fuss over "that little ice-cold bunch of land down there." Good question.

THEY DON'T BELIEVE IN FREEDOM OF SPEECH,

TRAFALGAR SQUARE NOTWITHSTANDING

Some Americans, having been inspired by the writings of Jeremy Bentham, John Locke, and John Stuart Mill, credit Britain with the invention of liberty as we know it. Clearly, these wiseacres aren't familiar with British laws on libel, the crime of intentionally damaging another's reputation. If you wish to sue people for talking smack about you in the United States, they're assumed to be innocent until you prove them to be guilty. In Britain, the reverse is true: Anyone can haul you before a judge for libel, and it's on you to prove that whatever you said about them was true and/or undamaging.

As a result, public conversation in Britain is as stale and underwhelming as parlor room chitchat. Whereas American audiences are treated to bold Bill O'Reillys and valiant Steven Colberts hurling invective and innuendo at those in power, British law puts a muzzle on the country's freest thinkers.

Americans believe the public realm consists of facts, objects, and dollars. Reputations are as inconsequential to us as ghosts. We are a thick-skinned people who can bear the brunt of assaults on our character without dragging our critics into court. Our bold policies abroad have shown that we care little what others may say or think of us now, for we are quite sure that history will bear out the validity of our cause.

YOU COULD FEED EVERY STARVING AFRICAN KID WITH THE MONEY THEY SPEND ON THEIR PALACES

Queen Elizabeth II spends her peoples' money faster than Imelda Marcos as Sacks. Last year, her family spent no less than £36.7 million in public money. That went to golf trips, hunting outings, skiing trips, coachmen, carriages, horses, handlers, the royal yacht, the maintenance of her family's numerous palaces, estates, and castles—and, of course, cases and cases of the driest gin. It does not include the millions of pounds in income earned by the royal family from their various landholdings and tourist admission fees, nor does the figure account for the royals' ability to live rent-free in such opulent surroundings where a workday consists of appearing at the balcony window to acknowledge the assembled crowds.

In 2005, Elizabeth II apparently thought this was a raw deal, as she negotiated with the local Westminster authorities to reduce the property tax on Buckingham Palace by £1 million. (Westminster City Council had little choice but to agree to this demand, because the Queen could theoretically choose not to pay any tax. She is, after all, the highest legal authority on the Isles of Evil.) I'll be the first to admit that some U.S. plutocrats have similar spending habits. But the difference is they did something to *earn* the money they spend, and they don't take food off the taxpayers' table for their chartered flights and luxury junkets.

THEY CAME UP WITH HARRY POTTER, BOY OCCULTIST

Any good churchgoing Brit will tell you that his country's pagan days are long gone, that his nation is a bastion of Christian piety. Then he'll go home, tuck his children into bed, and read them a tale of Harry Potter, the "boy wizard," the pagan who deals in magic and is but the latest attempt of the underground Druid elite to reestablish their credibility in the twenty-first century. The Potter books have now been translated into more than forty languages. A whopping three hundred million copies have sold worldwide. Each new title in the series is greeted with a blitz of publicity and widespread youth hysteria of Beatles-like intensity.

The main protagonist, Harry, has a mark in the shape of a lightning bolt on his forehead, perhaps a reference to the mark of the beast as described in the Book of Revelations. Those who do not practice the magical arts are derided as "muggles." Centaurs, giants, werewolves, and other creatures of pagan legend appear as a matter of course. At best, the Potter books are a bald-faced attempt to inflame America's Christian Right and further marginalize the role of religion and morality in America's popular culture. At worst, they are covert pagan propaganda, sugarcoated Satanisms intended to win impressionable young minds over to the spell-casters' cause.

THEY WORSHIP A GIANT CLOCK GOD AS THE LIVING, TICKING SYMBOL OF STATE AUTHORITY

It is normal for moldy old empires to try to ignore the passage of time. That way, they can pretend that the greatness of one hundred years prior has some bearing on the country today. But instead of ignoring time, Britons, strangely, worship it. At the heart of Britain is London. In the middle of London is the Palace of Westminster, home to the monarchy since Edward the Confessor and now the meeting place of Parliament as well. And the center of the palace, the holiest of British holiest, is a giant clock, the Great Clock, known to most as Big Ben.

Big Ben is a kind of secular clock god, symbolizing the eternal and absolute authority of the state apparatus. Whereas Americans prefer to keep time with their cell phones and wristwatches, Londoners look outward and upward, listening for the bells of the church steeples and straining their eyes to see Big Ben's hands.

Back in the days of the Industrial Revolution, on days when factory owners were struggling to fill a certain order, the greedy bosses were rumored to have bribed the clock keeper to slow Big Ben down a minute or two and so wring an extra drop of free labor out of their submissive and unquestioning employees. If Big Ben says it's two minutes to five, then two minutes to five it is, even if it was two minutes to five two minutes ago.

THEY ENCOURAGE
THE EATING OF MEAT

Environmentalist ninnies love to blame everything from global warming to decimated rainforests on the meatiness of the American diet. All those fast-food hamburgers, they say, fill up landfills, clog our arteries, and waste bushel upon bushel of precious corn, feed for animals that could have saved the lives of the starving huddled masses around the world. Good arguments, all, but they neglect to consider which civilization pioneered the eating of meat—not just as a fast-food snack, but at every meal—in the first place. It was, as you've likely guessed, the Evil Empire.

The British diet is one daylong meatfest. Morning begins with heaping plates of beans, eggs, pork, and beef. There are sausages, fried potatoes, and a hideous concoction called "blood pudding"—a blackened tube of barley, oatmeal, and congealed pigs' blood. Full of calories and deprived of any meaningful nutrients, your typical Englishman downs a plate of this greasy fare then grabs his umbrella and bowler hat and sleepwalks his way to work in a meat-induced coma of sorts. He must quaff tea throughout the day (English Breakfast, strong as gunpowder, is one workplace favorite) to keep from nodding off at his desk. Lunch is centered around oily slabs of cured meat held by two pieces of bread, a concoction called the "sandwich," named for the Earl of Sandwich, an eighteenth-century British lord who couldn't pull himself away from the gambling tables and so had to eat with his hands like a savage.

And so the hamburger as we know it today would never have come

into existence were it not for his lordship's inability to use a knife and fork. This bonanza of blood and tendons continues into the night, where supper climaxes with Beef Wellington, a meat-filled pastry dish, lamb shanks, and juicy sides of roast beef glistening under the knife of the host. Nothing pleases the eye of the British host more than the tender flesh of a dead, helpless animal dividing under the force of his knife. It reminds him of what it was once like to have the world at his mercy, served up on a porcelain plate.

THEY GAVE US LIAM
AND NOEL GALLAGHER,
BETTER KNOWN AS OASIS

While American musicians and artists are constantly seeking to outdo their predecessors, the Brits are a regressive and even decadent bunch. Knowing their best days are behind them, they repackage old postures and sounds ad nauseum and pray that the public won't notice. In the 1990s, the most flagrant attempt to pass off dated material as something new was Oasis, a band that more or less repeated the sound and look of the Beatles's career while setting aside the Fab Four's reputation for good behavior. Often resembling soccer hooligans or apolitical skinheads in their relentless boozing, brawling, and naked contempt for live audiences, Liam and Noel Gallagher learned quickly that the British public loves nothing more than prima donnas who mirror their own arrogant, imperial attitudes.

So they drank to excess, snorted coke, showed up or did not show up for gigs as they pleased, and periodically tried to clean themselves up enough to write a new suite of songs in the studio. They had a symbiotic and ultimately destructive relationship with the British tabloids, who feasted on the Gallaghers' bad behavior. The Gallaghers, in turn, felt obliged to outdo themselves, indulging in more depraved and even criminal behaviors with each subsequent tour.

The climax came in Munich, where Liam went on a drunken rampage, got his two front teeth knocked out, and wound up with a £35,000 fine from the German authorities. Britain may have lost her glorious empire, but her tradition of exporting violence is alive and well.

THEY THINK THEY WILL NEVER NEED A DENTIST, A DOCTOR, OR AN UNDERTAKER

The imperialists who conquered the globe for Britain, with their white pith helmets and spit-shined boots, liked to brag how "the sun never sets on the British Empire." Privately, many refused to come to terms with the fact that the sun would someday set on their own mortal bodies. They believed they were as invincible and ageless as the glorious trophies they carried back to the homeland. The scotch-swilling and cigar-puffing old boys of Eton would, in their own minds, live forever. They are the ones who started the wicked practice—an atrocity adopted by much of the developed world—of burying the dead in the greenest country fields beneath giant stone monuments, thus turning fine picnicking spots and playgrounds into acres of gated sorrows and solemnities.

Refusing to believe in their own inevitable demise, many British don't visit doctors or dentists on a regular basis. In 1945, *Time* magazine reported that one out of every eight British youths between the ages of sixteen and nineteen who visited the dentist needed not one or two or even five fillings, but a complete set of false teeth.

Six decades later, little has changed. The British still insist on drinking a pot of tea daily, which turns their pearly whites the color of moldy parchment. This dental trauma is magnified tenfold by the sugary scones, bon bons, and other seemingly innocent snacks that get dipped and swirled about with the tea. Whereas we Americans regularly go to the gym and happily pay out billions for the best health care known to man, the British start letting themselves go the day they're born. Their stiff upper lips are deployed to soldier through various tooth and body aches without medical aid, to conceal their rotting palates, and to maintain a sort of stoic grimace until the very moment when their souls are plucked from this Earth.

THEY INVENTED
COLLEGE

Up until the 1950s, the American people managed to stay blessedly free of the classism and striving that tends to characterize the imperial mindset. Then, just as the United States was reaching the height of its postwar powers to do battle with the Soviet Union, we succumbed to the allures of a social hierarchy, a stratified realm of grade point averages and standardized test scores where one's worth as a parent was judged solely by the school one's child was admitted to, and its ranking according to the hallowed list of *U.S. News and World Report.* After two hundred years of democratic love for our fellow man, snobbery managed to sneak into the United States under the cloak of that beloved British invention—college.

College, in its essence, is a place where learned men and women are allowed to spend their entire lives huddled inside libraries, earning generous salaries and leaves of absence without ever having to worry about how they'll do on their next performance review, or whether anyone will actually read their esoteric writings. Thanks to the generous tuition fees paid out by wave after wave of undergraduates, they've got a job for life. This system has its origins at Oxford and Cambridge and was imported to the States by American Anglophiles who wanted to start their own mini-Oxfords at Harvard, Yale, Princeton, and William and Mary.

With its powerful secret societies, rigid class lines, and greedy dons lounging in plush offices, college is still the most British of all American institutions, generally teaching American kids to read Marx and screw around on the Internet. I'd much prefer they learn something practical, like Terrorist Ass-Kicking 101.

THEY ENCOURAGE IMMODEST BEHAVIOR WITH THE MINISKIRT

AND OTHER LASCIVIOUS FASHIONS

After a century of having its sexual mores corseted and restrained by Victorian repression, Britain swung to the other extreme in the years following the second World War, indulging in decadent, drug-fueled orgies, casual sex, and brightly colored, revealing fashions that bordered on the depraved. Among the worst cases was the miniskirt, which served to forever alter a woman's legs from a utilitarian mode of transport into fetishized objects of seduction. Falling well above the knee and just below the point where the bottom of the buttocks meet the top of the thigh, the miniskirt distracts passersby from the business of the day, turning their thoughts toward prurient and lustful abandon.

The invention only becomes more perverse when one considers that British women are not especially known for their shapely legs. On the contrary, Twiggy, the British supermodel who did the most to popularize the miniskirt, was prized for her bony, sticklike figure. At its heart, the miniskirt was a final postwar push by Britain to reassert its imperial authority overseas. Having been deprived of its military and naval power, the Evil Empire could only attempt to dominate by projecting its twisted sense of fashion, music, and popular culture on the rest of the world.

THEY RUN THEIR PUBS
LIKE SOVIETS

The British pub had a reputation for being a dim, calming respite from the agonizing series of social performances and silent rituals of rank that form the daily routine of your run-of-the-mill Englishman. We are made to believe that after a few pints, stonemasons and aristocrats can throw their arms around one another's shoulders and join together in boisterous song. This is certainly true if you compare the pub atmosphere to the prickly air inside a London Tube car or in the middle of a long queue. But compared to the tranquil, unhurried refuge of the classic American dive bar, the British pub is as staid and formal as a debutante's ball.

First of all, there's no tipping. That's right: no tipping. If you decide to leave a pound sterling on the bar, nobody's going to turn you over to the bobbies, but the practice is frowned upon. No one is completely sure why the British don't tip their bartenders, but I suspect that after decades of rampant hopeless alcoholism among the middle and lower classes, it's a matter of economic necessity.

The result is what you would expect in an environment with no competition and no incentives—British barkeeps move at the speed of glaciers, and pubs get crowded as patrons are forced to stay for hours on end just to work up a decent buzz. Serving up twenty-ounce "imperial" pints doesn't make up for having to wait for the barman to finish reading the papers and chatting up the lasses to give you your next pour.

THEY TOOK THE SOUL
OUT OF ROCK & ROLL

During the Raj, the East India Company harvested India's native cotton and shipped it back to factories in Liverpool and Birmingham. There it was woven into cheap, mass-produced fabric and sold back to the Indians. The Raj ended in 1947, but an even more insidious form of mercantilism soon took its place, where British musicians would harvest classic forms of music perfected by the American working class, wring out album after album of cheap, imitative fluff, and market the watered-down result back to hapless American audiences. This tradition of befouling American airwaves begun by Sergeant Pepper's march up the charts continues today with Franz Ferdinand, Coldplay, the Arctic Monkeys, and other pieces of audio tripe. The very idea that there could be such a thing as a rock star was invented by the British press and their hunger to crown new royalty. The rock star is a god to be worshiped. He is a Lennon who is bigger than Jesus, a Jagger who may be Satan himself, a Beatle, one of the anointed, another debauched and self-aggrandizing royal whose misadventures are covered in breathless detail by the scandal-hungry hacks who man the Fleet Street presses.

Vain postures notwithstanding, these pretenders are the complete opposite of the original bluesman, who used music not as a tool to further his own celebrity but a salve to endure another day of being black, broke, and on the road. He had the one thing that money, amps, and tight pants can't get you, the thing that the British musical mercantilists couldn't pry from the soil of the Mississippi Delta: It's called soul. We got it. They don't.

THEY MADE FALSE PROMISES TO THE PALESTINIANS, INFURIATING THE ARAB WORLD

According to legend, the Trojan War began when Eris, goddess of discord, rolled a golden apple among a bickering trio of her fellow goddesses, who then enlisted armies of Greek and Trojan men to fight as their proxies. The ongoing conflict between the Jews and Palestinians has similar origins. Allah and Jehovah are cast as the Roman goddesses, the land of Israel is the golden apple they're fighting over, and the UK is the spiteful drama queen who set the whole ugly matter in motion. Jews and Muslims have had competing milk-and-honey landlust since biblical times, when, as the Old Testament tells, Jacob threw a tribe of idolaters out of the land of Canaan and claimed it for his people.

The British government, which had control of Palestine from 1917 to 1948, effectively threw gas on this centuries-old fire by first promising the land to the Jews with the Balfour Declaration of 1917, and then, one year later, declaring that the Holy Land's "indigenous peoples"—the Palestinians—also had a right to self-government. The next nine decades, as we all know, have been a mess of suicide bombings, bulldozed villages, and towering concrete walls. After being betrayed by

the British, the new Jewish state adopted a hostil
Lebanon, and its other Arab neighbors, forcing
spend billions trying to calm down yet another in.
hostilities were first kindled by British hands.

THEY HUNT SMART ANIMALS WITH DUMB ANIMALS, FOR SPORT

The days when pasty pith-helmeted colonels could hunt Zulu warriors on the Rhodesian grasslands are long gone, as are the days when you could take out a two-ton elephant with your blunderbuss, chop off the head, and get it stuffed and mounted for the wall of your country estate. Foxhunting, however, survives, as one of the last of Britain's great aristocratic bloodsports and an enduring symbol of her disregard for suffering, be it human or animal. It is a microcosm of British society at the height of the Evil Empire, showing how barbarism and supposedly enlightened ritual can coexist and even reinforce one another.

Most Americans are only acquainted with foxhunting through prints hung on the walls of department store haberdasheries. They imagine a troop of men in gallantly regimented dress blowing trumpets and deftly guiding their horses through the woods. What they don't see is what happens when the hounds finally apprehend the fox and tear the poor creature limb from limb like a rag doll. They call it "sport," but the fox is grossly outmatched, surrounded by hungry hounds and men on horseback.

Disguised as a pleasant country outing, foxhunting actually reenacts the animal sacrifices high Druid priests used to perform in prehistoric Britain, as evidenced by the ritual fox blood that orthodox huntmasters will smear on the cheeks of young hunters. How do M.P.s look in

the mirror after indulging in such needless cruelties and then criticize America's policy on the Guantanamo Bay detainees? Do they want a world where innocent foxes are killed for no reason while terrorists run free?

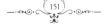

THEY INVENTED TABLOID JOURNALISM AND TURNED MICHAEL JACKSON INTO A CIRCUS FREAK

The word *tabloid* technically means a newspaper that opens sideways, like a magazine. Pioneered by British publishers in the early 1900s, tabloids are sensationalist weapons of mass distraction, emphasizing crimes, sporting events, and the doings of celebrities over straightforward hard news. Whereas the American press has always tried to unify a diverse continent by publishing news attractive to all, the British media uses newspaperdom to keep the various classes in their place.

Tabloids are the most debased of all newspaper forms, intended to fill the minds of the working classes with gossip and drivel. The most disturbing encounter the American people have had with the tabloids is the sad case of Michael Jackson, or "Jacko" as he's known to the Fleet Street hacks too lazy to type out his full name. By the time he pried the telescopic lenses of the British paparazzi off his face, he'd been bleached, stalked into hiding, and quite possibly driven mad. No one even cared about his private doings until the tabloids decided to make the poor man's troubles into a national obsession. In the last ten years, celebrity journalism has stretched its sickening tentacles across the Atlantic, appearing on American primetime television and magazines such as *US Weekly*. This is yet another way the old Evil Empire is attempting to rot our new one from the inside out.

THEY MADE SNOBBERY INTO SCIENCE

Only a Briton—Charles Darwin by name—could look at the animal world and see a "kingdom" of lords, ladies, princes, and paupers, whose fortunes were determined not by the vicissitudes of chance but by biological traits given to them at birth. Darwin, as we all know, theorized that evolution was driven by a process of natural selection. The bird with the bigger beak, for example, would beat the smaller-beaked birds in the race to suck worms out of the soil, killing off his competitors and ensuring that his big-beaked genes would be passed on.

Darwin's ideas were a hit not because they explained the natural world, but because they seemed to back up the Evil Empire's arrogant desire to "paint the map red" with hard science. Darwin was used to give the Evil Empire's progress the irresistible sheen of hard science, to lock every vassal state and penniless commoner into his place. According to the racist historians who ran with Darwin's ideas, Britain's dominance was not due to chance factors like the high oil and metal ore content in the soil, which guaranteed the Industrial Revolution would take place on their shores. Britain's success was coded (by God, perhaps) into the genes of her people. The Evil Empire had the right to enslave everyone else because Brits were better than everyone else.

Some call this science. I call it sickness.

THEY GAVE US THE FIRST MODERN SERIAL KILLER

Don't believe what you see on the History Channel—Jack the Ripper was not the world's very first serial killer. Hundreds of years before he stalked the streets of London, the retired French soldier Gilles de Rais tortured and killed hundreds of children from the surrounding countryside at the behest of an insane Italian counselor who was instructing him in the occult arts. Elizabeth Bathory, a Hungarian countess, took the lives of some six hundred young girls with the same entitlement and nonchalance that she might have desiccated a tin of fine bonbons.

But the world's most famous serial killer, the first to become a media sensation in the Jeffrey Dahmer or Charles Manson mode, was Jack the Ripper, who slashed the throats and dismembered the bodies of at least five prostitutes working London's shabby East End. The tragedy of the Ripper is his nickname—greedy Fleet Street press jockeys realized the public would buy more papers when killers were turned into twisted heroes. Ever since then, the psychos of the world have won no small measure of fame for their crimes, causing their already inflated sense of personal grandeur to balloon and likely inspiring them to take the lives of many more victims than they would have if they were operating in anonymity.

Yes, the bodies of dozens if not hundreds of innocents can be laid at the feet of British editors who will stop at nothing—not even granting eternal fame to twisted killers—to lure the public's attention.

THEY STARTED
THIS WHOLE
BLOOD FOR OIL THING

I like oil. Petroleum keeps our homes warm, our engines running, and I doubt we'll want to do without it in this lifetime. Oil equals industrial energy, which our rising American Empire needs in order to avoid going the way of the Evil one. In other words, oil is important, important enough that we shouldn't feel ashamed about fighting for it. That being said, if you don't think the oil under the sands of the Middle East is worth the blood of soldiers, don't blame Exxon or Shell or Halliburton. Blame Britain. Along with France, Britain was left with the responsibility of carving up the Middle East at the end of World War I.

First, they couldn't decide whether to promise modern-day Israel to the Palestinians or to the Jews. So they did both, and the Palestinians and Jews have been fighting ever since. Next, after the League of Nations handed the Empire the responsibility of building a stable national government in the brand-new country of Iraq, a fragment of the old Ottoman Empire, they rolled up their tents and declared the job over in 1947.

They were wrong. Over the next forty years, the country was taken over by a succession of military strongmen, ending with Saddam Hussein. In sum, when handed a sandy treasure chest filled with the better part of the planet's black gold, Britain proceeded to surround the treasure with volatile bombs, light the fuses, and walk away.

THEY ADORE PRISONS

Big Brother, as we all know, was the ruler of Oceania, the totalitarian dystopia described by British author George Orwell in his novel *1984*. Like most tyrants, Big Brother dominated the people with a combination of fear, lies, propaganda, and technology. Chief among his despotic devices was the telescreen, a video monitor that acted as a sort of one-way mirror between the citizen and the state, simultaneously broadcasting messages and observing the activities of the viewer.

Orwell was far from the first Englishman to imagine such a prison of continuous surveillance. He was merely following in the tradition of Jeremy Bentham, who came up with the fantastical and perverse Panopticon, which allowed one guard to monitor the activities of hundreds of prisoners by arranging their cells in a circular fashion around one central guard tower.

Lovers of law and punishment, the British have always relished doling out hard time. For hundreds of years, especially hated criminals were kept in the Tower of London, adjacent to rooms used for state business and storing the crown jewels. Would we chain convicts to the top of the Washington Monument? No, we spirit them off to supermax lockups on desolate river islands or surrounded by hundreds of miles of desert. Every civilization has its prisons, but few have inflicted punishment on the convict hordes with the same relish as the Evil Empire.

THEY GOT
OSAMA BIN LADEN
ALL RILED UP

In the 1980s, Osama bin Laden was all about the United States of America. His valiant mujahideen helped us kick the Russians out of Afghanistan, a campaign forever memorialized by Sylvester Stallone in *Rambo III*. His family invested some of their vast wealth in Arbusto, George W.'s first Texas oil venture, as well as the Bush-friendly Carlyle Group. So what happened? Where did this reliably anti-Commie trust-fund rebel go wrong? To understand the roots of bin Laden's hatred, we must go back to his first contact with Westerners. These were the teachers who taught him English at his prestigious high school in Saudi Arabia, and they were not Americans, but Brits and Irishmen. Later on, he and many of his brothers would take pleasure trips and summer courses near London. An early photograph of bin Laden at Oxford in 1971 shows a gangly-limbed youth, completely freaked out by the swinging sexual decadence surrounding him. Like any visitor to the Isles, he was assaulted on all sides by vain placards, monuments, and parades, many of which were in honor of the slaughter of thousands of Muslims on the sands of the former Ottoman Empire.

But there was a problem—the British Empire had already more or less imploded. Bin Laden had been born too late to extract the revenge he so intensely desired. It was then that he began to formulate his theory of "the West," which lumps the United States and Britain together. He adopted the anti-Western teachings and murderous ideology of the writer Sayyid Qutb, who struggled to liberate Egypt from British influence throughout the 1950s. Bin Laden chose to ignore the fact that Britain is a Christian nation and America is a secular melting pot, and that we were busy building railroads while they were mowing down Ottomans by the hundreds in hails of machine gun fire.

THEY WANT TO KICK PADDY ROY BATES OFF HIS OWN PRIVATE ISLAND

Royalty is a farce. The thing that makes the royals royal isn't their pedigree or their coat of arms or the blue blood supposedly flowing through their veins but gall, plain and simple—the gall to stand up and claim that they're better than the rest of their countrymen. Behind the palaces, mottos, and ministers is an old lady claiming she's a queen and a few thousand career bureaucrats whose livelihoods depend on the rest of the British nation believing her. In a country built around such loose notions of sovereignty, seizing the privileges of monarchy for yourself is the equivalent of printing phony $100 bills.

So when Paddy Roy Bates, a former major in the British Army, proclaimed himself king of Sealand, a small, abandoned island in international waters off the coast of the UK, he was met with stubborn resistance from British diplomats. Bates's island wasn't an island in the palm tree and sand sense, but an abandoned concrete platform used by British helicopters during World War II. Bates printed his own stamps, minted his own coins, sold titles and honours over the Internet, fired on armed British military vessels looking to take his platform back, and even fought off a German saboteur who wanted to kidnap the royal Bates family and seize Sealand for himself.

But while Sealand is now diplomatically recognized as a sovereign nation by Germany and France, the UK still refuses to acknowledge

its existence. It would seem Britain wants to be the only island in the North Atlantic with eccentric, overreaching monarchies. Or maybe they just hate rugged individualists, the spirited rebels among us who realize that sovereignty isn't some exclusive domain of the privileged but a universal inheritance that anyone can find floating in the middle of the ocean.

THEY PUT SADDAM HUSSEIN IN POWER

Surely you recall the film *Lawrence of Arabia?* It tells the legend of Lawrence, a golden-haired and limp-wristed colonist-hero, who led the Allied campaign in the Middle East during World War I. Lawrence went native and trained the desert nomad Hussein family in the art of British warfare while his colleague, Harry St. John Philby, trained the House of Saud. Their goal was to drive the crumbling Ottoman Empire out of the Middle East and gain unfettered access to Mesopotamia's succulent oil reserves.

The British, as was their habit in the Middle East, made promises they couldn't keep, pledging control of the entire Middle East and Mecca, the Muslim holy city, to both families. When the war ended, the Saudis got Mecca and Saudi Arabia. The Saudi patriarch was paid a retainer of £3,000 a month to get out of the way and keep that oil flowing. The Husseins got Jordan and Iraq and vague promises of British assistance, which failed to materialize after the country was taken over by the Ba'ath Party. The leader of the Ba'aths, Saddam Hussein, was of no relation to the original Anglo-loving Husseins, and Lawrence's training did little to keep him from conquering the desert tribes.

That's the British for you. They'll fight tooth and nail beside our boys in the trenches, but once that mustard gas clears, they'll refuse to lift a finger to stop a third of the world's known oil reserves from falling into the hands of a mustachioed madman.

THEY PUT PRINCESS DI
IN HARM'S WAY

The British public always had a morbid fascination with Diana Spencer, Princess of Wales. Maybe it was her golden hair, or her Aryan good looks, or her embodiment of the secret British wish that common people might aspire to the same graces and privileges of the monarchy, though Diana, the daughter of an earl, was far from common. Whatever the reason, Diana was, as Tony Blair put it, "the people's princess," and the people couldn't get enough of current Diana news, gossip, and, most of all, photographs. They loved her dearly, and they may have even loved her to death.

In August 1997, divorced Diana was staying at the Paris Ritz with the playboy Dodi Fayed. That evening, they left the hotel in Fayed's Mercedes, chased by eight French paparazzi hungry for shots that could fetch thousands of pounds from the British tabs. They entered an underground tunnel at about sixty miles per hour—twice the legal limit—crashed into a pole, and died.

Britain went into mourning, with the media, the Queen, and the philandering Prince of Wales all giving themselves long hard looks in the mirror and wondering what might have been done to prevent this tragedy. Never, however, has the British public come to terms with the fact that her death was driven by their demand for pictures, and the Evil Empire's immoderate appetite for tabloid news continues to go unchecked.

THEY LEFT AFRICA TOO WEAK TO FIGHT OFF AIDS

Africa is AIDS central, home to the majority of the forty million people now infected with the HIV virus. If you look at a map of where the AIDS pandemic is at its worst, it looks almost exactly like the Evil Empire at its height, with big black blotches around the Cape of Good Hope and sub-Saharan regions. This is not a coincidence. The countries that have been hit the worst by AIDS are those countries whose health infrastructure, schools, and economies languished under British colonial rule. Britain didn't intend for Africa to be devastated by a viral epidemic, but the Crown's refusal to train their colonial subjects in ways of self-government left Africa unable to administer AIDS programs after they left.

Today, guilt-ridden British rock stars try to make up for historical injustices with Band Aid and Live Aid programs, but these well-intentioned charity tours can hardly heal the wounds English officers inflicted on the continent at the start of the century. Former French colonies, on the other hand, have fought AIDS with a Magic Johnson–like resiliency.

THEY STILL
WON'T LET GO

B ritain needs to give it up! Time and rebellion have shrunk their Evil Empire down to a plateful of moldy leftovers. Their cultural dominance is a thing of the past. America has made Britain an understudy, a vassal.

Yet rather than accept their place in this new world order, Britain continues to demand seats at the G-8, the UN Security Council, and around other tables with the nations that actually control the globe, as though they were still a great power. They even tend to a dusty arsenal of nuclear weapons, just in case. You can take away the Queen's empire, apparently, but you can't take away her pride. America and China, the world's truly great powers, need to stop the dangerous practice of humoring our bitter, failed ally.

Given the havoc that British arms wreaked on the world for the last two hundred years, do we really want them stockpiling weapons of mass destruction? Why not err on the safe side, and follow the Condoleezza Rice method: imposing economic sanctions until they disarm, and seeing where things go from there?

THEY MADE MODERN ART INTO A CIRCUS FREAKSHOW

Who but Damien Hirst, an ambitious young British art school student, would have the nerve to submerge a dead shark in a tank of formaldehyde, call it *The Physical Impossibility of Death in the Mind of Someone Living*, and sell the resulting abomination as art?

And who but Charles Saatchi, the famed British adman, would have the gall to buy such a thing and then bankroll the next ten years of Hirst's career? Not just Hirst's career, actually, but those of his equally pretentious Goldsmiths College buddies as well, allowing them to hang out all day smoking cigarettes in their studio spaces, spend Saatchi's money, and earn notoriety as the Young British Artists, or YBAs. Despite millions of pounds in patronage from Saatchi—who perhaps saw his own lack of craft and technique mirrored in the crudely storyboarded showpieces of these shock-art clowns—Hirst still had difficulties building anything that would last for the ages.

Since first being dipped in formaldehyde circa 1991, chunks of his $12 million shark have begun to rot and break off faster than the Royal Navy under U-Boat fire. And it smells.

THEY CAN'T DANCE

The British lack of rhythm is well known to anyone who has attended a London nightclub and discovered the great mass of patrons standing on the sidelines nursing their cocktails while a few especially intoxicated individuals jerk about spasmodically in the middle of the dance floor, more or less oblivious to the beat.

But if you really want to see the Evil Empire's awkwardness on display, take a look at the stiff-legged and straight-backed Morris folk dancers as they perform their cute little "jigs" up and down the town square, hopping and skipping without an ounce of swing or soul in their hips. You might think that more than four hundred years of traditional Morris dancing would have imparted some fluidity or form to their moves, but accompanied by a fiddle and an accordion, a Brits joints tend to twitch with the same robotic jerkiness as a rusted marionette. Morris dancing has survived because of its martial and mechanical nature. It is as strict, ritualized, and meaningless as the various courtesies and social performances the Englishman is expected to undertake throughout his day.

The practice is so sad and dull that children could not bear to sit through it were it not for the elaborately costumed fools and beasts who break up the strict order of the Morris troupes with mascot-like pranks.

THEY DROVE THE ABORIGINES FROM DREAMTIME BLISS TO DRUNKEN POVERTY

Until 1769, when Captain James Cook spotted it through his spyglass, Australia looked a lot like paradise. Koala bears snacked contentedly on the leaves on the eucalyptus tree, and aborigines gently floated through life in Dreamtime, a stunningly enlightened theological construct where the past, the present, the future, the living, and the dearly departed come together to form the present moment.

But Cook saw Australia as just another piece of dirt to sink his Union Jack into. Over the next 250 years or so, in a series of epidemics, forced migrations, and outright massacres, the Australian aborigine population was reduced from 350,000 to 50,000. Corralled into crowded camps and deprived of the right to vote until 1963, native Australians were never given their own casinos so they could make a proper go of it in industrial society. Instead they live off the dole, rarely working or attending school, and are only able to access their fabled Dreamtime by liquoring themselves into a stupor. Granted, America's treatment of our native people was more than insensitive, but we look like excellent neighbors when compared with the Evil Empire.

THEY CORRUPTED
THE FINE ART
OF ADVERTISING

No one knows better than I do that today's advertising puts a premium on colorful illusion, the aggressive pursuit of the consumer in every quarter of his life, and long, elegant trails of little white lies, fibs that this action figure flies on its own, that one pass of this handy disposable mop will return your wooden floor to its original glory, that one dollop of this fancy chemical will undo the clog in your drain, etc. That's advertising for you. Not untrue, exactly, but not completely true either.

We have an Englishman to thank for these tricky textual shenanigans, a man by the name of David Ogilvy, who singlehandedly turned advertising from the plainspoken and straightforward price-item-description formula of the nineteenth century to the Super Bowl of shimmering sock puppets we know today. Ogilvy's "Magic Lantern" sales presentations prefigured PowerPoint's mindless and authoritative cognitive style. So the next time you're forced to look at a hot babe pushing a razor with seven blades or sit in a dark room and stare at pie charts, blame the English.

THEY MADE SOCCER INTO THE WORLD'S GAME

Soccer is a British invention, devised, codified, and then popularized by British schoolboys for the purposes of lunchtime amusement. In its original form, soccer, American football, and rugby were all the same thing, just a big mess of men on a grassy field scrambling in the mud for a leather ball. There were no shin guards, no red or yellow cards, no refs. The highest purpose of play was to prepare young people for war, and by this yardstick, the original lawless soccer was ideal.

Then, as always, came the weak-willed worriers and lily-livered legislators, who introduced the use of pads and officials and divided this glorious full-body game into two games. One, rugby, got the pushing, shoving, and carrying elements. The other, soccer, got the dribbling and the better part of the kicking.

Given the aversion of the English to hard-nosed physical contact, soccer quickly surpassed rough-and-tumble rugby in popularity. Imperial taskmasters taught the seductively mild game to their colonial subjects in India and Africa. It sapped their rebel energies and taught them, match by match, to be docile, cooperative subjects.

THEY CAN'T DEAL WITH HIP-HOP CULTURE

At some point during the decade that elapsed between Vanilla Ice and Eminem, white America got down with its black self. The public at large accepted that our national tapestry would be far stiffer and blander without its black and brown threads. African Americans, once confined to the stage and the basketball court, were given unprecedented access to the inner sanctums of popular culture. Afternoon talk shows. The evening news. Nothing was off limits. Hip-hop fashion and slang shed their racial identities to join the mainstream. Everyone, from Al Roker to suburban moms, kicked around words like *dis'* and *bling* as though Ebonics were their mother tongue.

The British, on the other hand, still see the world in the antiquated terms of highbrow and lowbrow. They completely freaked out when hip-hop culture started to catch on and cross color lines. Rather than indulging their kids' cutting-edge desires for gold chains and velour Rocawear tracksuits, they invented a new slur with which to castigate them—*chav.* The direct descendant of *yobbo, casual,* and other terms of Anglo-racio-classist derision, *chav* suggests that sneakers and jewelry make a Brit less of a Brit.

No longer able to look down her nose at the rest of the world, the Evil Empire now resorts to looking in the mirror and seeing its most colorful citizens as warts on the royal visage.

THEY'RE BEHIND GLOBAL WARMING

Coal is nasty stuff. Tiny particles of it get stuck in miners' lungs, gradually cutting off the flow of oxygen to the blood. It burns hot but dirty, blackening and corroding whatever is in its path. What's worse, burning coal releases noxious CO_2 into the atmosphere, a greenhouse gas that lets the sun's rays into our atmosphere but won't let them back out. In the eighteenth and nineteenth centuries, Britain designed the entire Industrial Revolution around engines that ran on steam heated by coal as well as coke, coal's fiery cousin.

It didn't have to be this way. We could have stuck with wood furnaces and water wheels, or just waited a few years until solar power hit the scene. Guiltiest of all was James Watt, whose popular steam engine proved indispensable to manufacturers and who set the world irrevocably down the coal-lined path to destruction. But because the Brits were so impatient to get those factory fires burning hot right then, we may be stuck with a few centuries of floods, hurricanes, and coastal towns being drowned in the rising tide.

Today, there is nearly a ton of coal burned each year for every man, woman, and child on Earth. Never before in the planet's 400,000 years of history have carbon dioxide levels been half as high. Living on a cold, dreary island protected from rising water levels by high cliffs, the British will never have to experience the ill effects of the planetary destruction they have wrought.

THEY MADE ELTON JOHN
A KNIGHT

E lton John always loved attention. He chose the piano, a solo instrument, and gave himself such peacocking aliases as "Pinball Wizard" and "Captain Fantastic." But his career of limelight-hogging pretension reached its climax in 1995, when Queen Elizabeth II made this toothsome fairy a knight of the British Empire. No longer was he merely Elton John. Even though most of his swordplay was of the steam room variety, and his only valorous service to Britain was depressing a series of black and white keys for the amusement of his countrymen, he was now Sir Elton John CBE, Commander of the British Empire.

Knighthood is but one part of a larger system known as "honours," through which the monarchy seeks to ingratiate itself with everyone from Steven Spielberg to General Norman Schwarzkopf, Middle Eastern princes, and aging rock stars. It is an attempt to make the entire world of power and celebrity bow down before the majesty of the crown, otherwise known as the "fount of honour," and gradate their achievement according to a royal formula of titles, medals, and privileges. There are barons, dames, ladies, and knights. There are even "life peers," a title that permits its bearer to join the House of Lords. Just imagine an American president who thought he could personally mint senators by touching his old college buddies on the shoulder with a sword.

The American people wouldn't stand for such naked inequality under the law. But the British are in such thrall before her royal majesty that even the counterculture buys into her system of meaningless rewards.

THEY GO WHEREVER THE GOLD IS

What accounts for the bad treatment the Australian Dreamtimers received at the hands of their British guests? Perhaps it was because the crown designated Australia the Evil Empire's penal colony, to be populated exclusively by 162,000 convicted criminals from Britain. It was these thieves, killers, madmen, and assorted thugs who gave the poor aboriginals their first taste of western civilization.

All this changed in 1841, when the Reverend William Branwhite Clarke struck gold. Over the next thirty years, the British population on the Australian continent quadrupled to just over 1.7 million. The diligence with which these greedy prospectors attempted to sniff out ore earned Australian soldiers the nickname "digger," which came in handy during World War I when their British cousins in Parliament were only too happy to send them into the trenches against Kaiser Wilhelm's men. Once the royals got a taste of Australian gold, they never let go. In a little-known ruse that continues to this day, the monarchy maintains its hold on Australia, claiming a full quarter of their flag and hailing the Queen of England as the Queen of Australia as well.

THEY SLICED NORTH AMERICA ACROSS THE MIDDLE

Immediately after the Revolutionary War, Canada received thousands of United Empire Loyalists, American colonists who wanted to continue to offer their loyalty to the evil crown. Ever since, Britain has fed the Canadian stereotype of the ugly American as a heavy-handed, egotistical buffoon, all the while whispering in America's ear that Canadians are too weak-willed and outside of the global power loop to ever become full partners in the world community. Their plan for North America is the same as it ever was: divide and conquer.

Britain secretly fears that Canada might replace them as America's best friend, or worse, join the United States in a glorious continental union. These worries grew more intense after the passage of NAFTA. So the Brits formed their own special club—the European Union. Americans need to stop making fun of Canadians and start showing them the respect they deserve—for their winter-hardened constitutions, their delicious lagers, and their enviably cheap health care system. It's about time we stop taking pains to please a frigid island nation and start learning from our neighbors to the north.

THEY'RE SCREWING UP
THE WAR ON TERROR

When bin Laden flew those airplanes into the towers, my fellow Americans and I were pissed. Someone had to pay. We were more than happy to fly out to the Middle East by ourselves and start rounding up civilization's enemies. We'd happily spend our own money and send our own young men to get the revenge we sorely craved. All we needed was a friend, a buddy country to nominally turn our unilateral effort into a "coalition." We needed a partner, someone to help us put on a pleasant dog-and-pony show for the international community.

But Britain, you couldn't even give us that, could you? Tony Blair's literalism and weak-willed internationalism forced us to invade Iraq on the pretext of "Weapons of Mass Destruction," when what we really wanted was regime change with a side of holy crusader vengeance. Even more of a nuisance than Blair himself were the touchy British people, who seemed to want our mission to fail the day it began. While most of the American people stood solidly behind the War on Terror, measures to impeach Blair and/or try him for "war crimes" made serious headway in the United Kingdom. Odd behavior for a country that spent most of the last two hundred years imposing its will on the rest of the world.

Instead of complaining, England ought to be grateful that our troops are out there sweating in the desert heat, cleaning up the despotic mess they made of the Middle East.

THEY OWE
THE WORLD BIG

Here's the American legal code in a nutshell: Whenever somebody's hurt, somebody else is to blame. And whoever's to blame had better open up their wallet and pay. In court, this comes in the form of damages. In world affairs, it comes in the form of reparations. Paying reparations is like putting on the dunce hat when you screw up in class. It's healthy. It's humbling. It helped get the Germans and the Japanese back on the right track after World War II.

And, after a millennium of trickery, theft, murder, and the countless other misdeeds cataloged herein, it's high time that Britain pay as well. That's justice, American style.

The bill you see to the right is far from complete. It ignores the plight of the Dutch Boers, overlooks the Indian Raj, and fails to take into account the financial and emotional distresses suffered by Irish, American, Canadian, and Australian subjects when gripped by the iron hand of British rule. But these five items do start to give a general idea of just how much Britain owes to the world:

INVOICE OF REPARATIONS PAYABLE ON RECEIPT

To:
Queen Elizabeth II
Buckingham Palace
London, UK

First Iraq War: . . . . $71 billion
(as estimated by the Department of Defense)

Second Iraq War: . . . . $282 billion+
(as calculated by Congressional Appropriations)

Total Cost of Slavery: . . . . $7.7 trillion
(one percent of the sum demanded by the African World Reparations Committee)

Opium War Refund: . . . . $28.8 trillion
($21 million extorted from China through the Treaty of Nanking in 1842,
with interest, compounded annually)

Versailles Refund: . . . . $21.6 trillion
($26 billion extorted from defeated German government after
World War I, with interest, compounded annually)

TOTAL REPARATIONS DUE:
$58,400,000,000,000 or £31,960,000,000,000

Please Remit IMMEDIATELY to:
Steven A. Grasse, Philadelphia, U.S.A.
For Immediate Disbursement to the Afflicted Subject Peoples of the World
Sign the petition at www.britishreparations.org

Not to worry, Britain. I know paying off such a sum would bankrupt you. And though I do hold something of a grudge, I would never want to see your people reduced to angry poverty. Two wrongs don't make a right.

So I'm not expecting to see a check any time soon.

But could we at least get a simple "Thank you, America"?

Or even a "Thank you for flying all over the world, cleaning up the smoking remains of our Evil Empire"?

Or, maybe, at the very least, "Thanks for picking up the tab for us, mates. We'll pay you back when we get it"?

It would be a good start.

ABOUT THE AUTHOR

STEVEN A. GRASSE is the founder and CEO of a prominent independent advertising agency in Philadelphia. His firm is credited with more or less inventing modern day "guerrilla" and "buzz" marketing. He perfected these two techniques by founding and promoting his own brands, such as G-Mart, Bikini Bandits, and Sailor Jerry. Steven has also produced and directed several feature-length independent films, as well as music videos for artists such as A Perfect Circle, Dee Dee Ramone, and the Eagles of Death Metal.

Steven's ancestors first came to America back in the early 1600s to escape British persecution and have been striking back against their oppressors for hundreds of years. They have fought in every major U.S. conflict, including the Revolutionary War and the War of 1812, both against the British. This is his first book, and given the Brits' thin skins and their adeptness at manipulating history, he will not be surprised if it turns out to be his last.

PENNY RIMBAUD is an author, poet, performance artist, and cultural terrorist. He is perhaps best known for being the drummer, lyricist, and cofounder of the seminal anarchist band Crass. Crass was a product of Dial House, the free-thinking open house in Essex, England, that Rimbaud founded in the late sixties and still makes his home. Throughout his long creative life, Rimbaud has been fearlessly outspoken in his criticism both of the past and present brutalities, hypocrisies, and arrogances of his native United Kingdom.

THE END